Kooky Crochet

Kooky Crochet

30 Remarkably Wacky Projects

Linda Kopp

LARK BOOKS
A Division of
Sterling Publishing Co., Inc.
New York

Editor:
Linda Kopp

Development Editor:
Terry Taylor

Art Director:
Kristi Pfeffer

Cover Designer:
Cindy LaBreacht

Technical Consultant:
Karen J. Hay

Assistant Editor:
Susan Kieffer

Associate Art Director:
Shannon Yokeley

Art Production Assistant:
Jeff Hamilton

Editorial Assistance:
Mark Bloom
Cassie Moore

Hair & Makeup:
E. Scott Thompson

Illustrator:
Orrin Lundgren

Photographer:
Stewart O'Shields

Library of Congress Cataloging-in-Publication Data

Kopp, Linda, 1960-
  Kooky crochet : 30 remarkably wacky projects / Linda Kopp. -- 1st ed.
      p. cm.
  Includes index.
   ISBN-13: 978-1-57990-978-9 (pb-trade pbk. : alk. paper)
   ISBN-10: 1-57990-978-7 (pb-trade pbk. : alk. paper)
   1. Crocheting--Patterns. I. Title.
   TT820.K755 2007
   746.43'4041--dc22

                                        2006101484

10 9 8 7 6 5 4 3 2 1

First Edition

Published by Lark Books, A Division of
Sterling Publishing Co., Inc.
387 Park Avenue South, New York, N.Y. 10016

Text © 2007, Lark Books
Photography © 2007, Lark Books unless otherwise specified
Illustrations © 2007, Lark Books unless otherwise specified

Distributed in Canada by Sterling Publishing,
c/o Canadian Manda Group, 165 Dufferin Street
Toronto, Ontario, Canada M6K 3H6

Distributed in the United Kingdom by GMC Distribution Services,
Castle Place, 166 High Street, Lewes, East Sussex, England BN7 1XU

Distributed in Australia by Capricorn Link (Australia) Pty Ltd.,
P.O. Box 704, Windsor, NSW 2756 Australia

If you have questions or comments about this book, please contact:
Lark Books
67 Broadway
Asheville, NC 28801
(828) 253-0467

Manufactured in China

ISBN 13: 978-1-57990-978-9
ISBN 10: 1-57990-978-7

For information about custom editions, special sales, premium and corporate
purchases, please contact Sterling Special Sales Department at 800-805-5489 or
specialsales@sterlingpub.com.

Contents

Introduction 6

Kitsch for Home & Self
Cronuts and Crochagels 10
Mixed Grill Place Mats 13
Hyperbolic Ball 20
Amigurumi Birds 22
Catch of the Day 25
Boa Ball Kitty Toy 28
Sunnyside Up Potholder 30
Fortune Kookies 33
Fuzzy Dice Pillow 36
Tadpole Friends 38
Find Your Cocktail Coasters 41
Monster Puppet Pals 44
Mossy Zen Rock Garden 48

Wacky Wearables
Luche Libre Ski Mask 54
Medusa Skullie 58
Diva Flip-Flops 62
Eve's Fig Leaf Halter 66
Haute Hardware Leg Warmers
& Glovelets 70
Bunches of Blobble Belts 73

Mapcap Accessories
Funky Felted Laptop Bag &
PSP Cozy 78
Coffee Service for One 82
Bag of Armor 86
Two-Liter Purse 88
Emoticon Bag 92
Skull and Crossbones Appliqués 96
Summer Hat and Tote Combo 100
Convertible Hat/Purse 103

Gallery 106
Designer Bios 112
Stitches & Techniques 116
Acknowledgments 124
Index 126

Introduction

Are you up to your eyeballs in crocheted scarves? Have you stitched up hats for all your friends, each family member, and even some passing acquaintances? Do you long for projects with more imagination, more originality, more sheer fun? Welcome to the creative world of Kooky Crochet, where attitude is as important as technique and sometimes the only real purpose of a project is playful—or irreverent—self-expression.

Take the crocheted donuts or bagels, for example. You can stitch up a dozen of these clever curios—complete with frosting and sprinkles. They're full of fiber and make a low-cal table decoration. Tired of those disappointing fortune cookie predictions? Rule your own destiny by penning brilliantly optimistic predictions and popping them into crocheted Fortune Kookies. The popularity of Japanese anime is sweeping the globe, and its influence can be seen in the cute-as-a-button Amigurumi Bird and Tadpole companion projects. Or give a nod to more traditional Japanese culture and crochet a soul-soothing desktop Zen Rock Garden.

Useful items aren't out, but why not make them artistic statements while you're at it? Like potholders and oven mitts—yup, things get hot, gotta have 'em. But how about using a fish oven mitt made from batik fabric strips to take your brownies out of the oven? When things get cold, instead of a ho-hum ski mask, crochet up a manly Luche Libre Mask, guaranteed to fight any head colds and perhaps capture the attention of the local law enforcement. And really, can you ever have too many handbags? Once you've guzzled that two-liter bottle of soda, we'll show you how to fashion the empty container into an edgy purse that's "clearly" unique.

Using creative materials is also a part of the Kooky Crochet credo. Try the urban chic Bag of Armor—a virtually indestructible carryall, thanks to its crocheted construction of rugged poly strapping tape (available at your local hardware store in fashionable black or gray). Or how about doing something with those plastic grocery bags that seem to multiply like rabbits? The environmentally friendly Summer Tote and Hat Combo puts those pesky bags to good use while yielding funky, waterproof accessories. Recycle and be stylish!

For those who suffer from a short attention span, have demanding schedules, or are just dipping their toes into the proverbial ocean that is crochet, we've got you covered with quick and easy-as-pie projects like the Fuzzy Dice Pillow, Meowabeau Puffs (a kitty's delight), and the fascinating Hyperbolic Ball. And for your crocheting convenience, you'll find a handy reference guide of stitches and techniques in the back of the book.

You hold in your hand your passport to a new crochet galaxy—one of all your own making. Be fearless! Explore your creativity! Astound your friends! Baffle the unimaginative! Soon you'll look at everything in a different way. Who knows…you may never go back to scarves and hats again.

Kitsch
for Home & Self

Home Kitschy Home. Be it ever so kooky.

Cronuts and Crochagels

(aka Crocheted Donuts and Bagels)

What are yummy, rich, and calorie-free?
Crocheted bagels and donuts, of course.
Make a dozen in a variety of flavors
to decorate your table, amuse
your dieting friends, and use up
luscious yarn scraps. The ends
of single crochet tubes are
joined to form each bagel
or donut; then high-fiber
raisins, nuts, frosting, and
sprinkles are added.
100% Fiberlicious!

Designer: **Myra Wood**

SKILL LEVEL
Easy

FINISHED MEASUREMENT
About 5"/12.5cm diameter

FOR ONE DONUT OR BAGEL
YOU WILL NEED
Approx 70yd/64m bulky weight yarn, bagel or donut color (A)

Approx 25yd/23m worsted weight yarn, frosting color (for donut only) (B)

Approx 2yd/2m worsted weight yarn, variety of flavor or sprinkle colors (C)

Hook: 4.5mm/G-7 or size needed to obtain gauge

YARN NEEDLE
2oz/56g polyester fiberfill

STITCHES USED
Chain (ch)
Double crochet (dc)
Half double crochet (hdc)
Single crochet (sc)
Slip stitch (sl st)

SPECIAL TECHNIQUES
French knot (page 122)

GAUGE
Gauge is not crucial.
12 sc and 10 rnds sc = 4"/10cm.

BAGEL OR DONUT BASE
With A, leaving a 4"/10cm yarn tail, ch 16, sl st in first ch to form a ring.

Rnd 1: Ch 1, sc in each ch around; do not join; work0 proceeds in continuous spiral (16 sc).

Work progresses in continuous spiral; do not join rounds (unless otherwise instructed). Mark beginning of first round and move marker as each new round is started.

Rnd 2: Sc in each sc around.

Repeat Rnd 2 until tube measures 11"/28cm. Sl st in next st after end of last round. Fasten off, leaving a 7"/18cm yarn tail for sewing.

ASSEMBLY
Stuff the tube with fiberfill until it is packed full from end to end.

Tie the two yarn tails together and thread longer tail onto yarn needle.

Sew one open tube end to the other, matching stitch for stitch around as close as possible. Turn tube as needed to sew smoothly. Weave in ends.

With B, ch 20, sl st in first ch to form a ring.

Rnd 1: Ch 1, sc in each ch around; join with sl st in first st (20 sc).

Rnds 2 and 3: Ch 1, sc in each st around; join with sl st in first st.

Rnd 4: Ch 1, * sc in next 3 sts, 2 sc in next st; repeat from * around; join with sl st in first st (25 sc).

Rnd 5: Ch 1, * sc in next 4 sts, 2 sc in next st; repeat from * around; join with sl st in first st (30 sc).

Rnd 6: Ch 1, * sc in next 5 sts, 2 sc in next st; repeat from * around; join with sl st in first st (35 sc).

Rnd 7: Ch 1, * sc in next 6 sts, 2 sc in next st; repeat from * around; join with sl st in first st (40 sc).

Rnd 8: Ch 1, * sc in next 7 sts, 2 sc in next st; repeat from * around; join with sl st in first st (45 sc).

Rnd 9: Ch 1, * sc in next 8 sts, 2 sc in next st; repeat from * around; join with sl st in first st (50 sc).

Rnd 10: Ch 1, 2 sc in next st, sc in

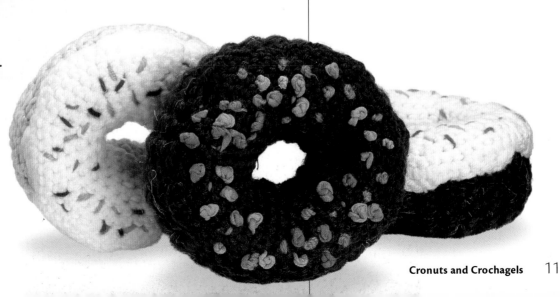

next 8 sts, 2 sc in next st, * sc in next 9 sts, 2 sc in next st; repeat from * around; join with sl st in first st (56 sc).

Rnd 11: Ch 1, * sc in next st, hdc in next st, dc in next 3 sts, hdc in next st, sc in next st; repeat from * around; join with sl st in first st. Fasten off, leaving a 20"/51cm yarn tail for sewing.

Sprinkles *(optional)*

With C, sew small straight stitches randomly on top of icing.

FINISHING

With C, sew small stitches and French knots on top of Bagel for each flavor as desired.

Place Frosting on top of Donut, tucking center smoothly into donut hole. Sew both open edges of frosting to donut.

Weave in ends.

This project was created with

1 skein each of Lion Brand's Homespun, 98% acrylic, 2% polyester, 6oz/170g = 185yd/169m, color #326 Ranch (cinnamon raisin bagel), color #380 Fawn (sesame and poppy seed bagel), #381 Barley (pumpernickel raisin bagel), #790 Shaker (everything bagel), #309 Deco (plain donut)

1 skein each of Lion Brand's Wool-Ease Thick & Quick, 80% acrylic, 20% wool, 6oz/170g = 106yd/97m, color #404 Wood (chocolate donut).

Mixed Grill Place Mats

If you aim to set a festive table for your next cookout, start by setting the mood with place mats featuring cookout favs. Whether it's burgers, wieners, kabobs, or T-bones on the grill, these whimsical place mats are sure to amuse your barbeque buddies.

Designer:
Regina Rioux Gonzalez

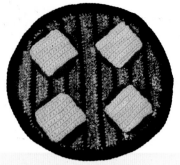

FINISHED MEASUREMENT

16"/41cm diameter

YOU WILL NEED (FOR ONE SET OF FOUR PLACE MATS)

Approx 420yd/384m worsted weight wool yarn, coal color (A)

Approx 420yd/384m worsted weight wool yarn, grill color (B)

Approx 50yd/46m worsted weight wool yarn, steak and tomato red (C)

Approx 50yd/46m worsted weight wool yarn, steak and onion white (D)

Approx 30yd/27m worsted weight wool yarn, frankfurter and meat cube rust (E)

Approx 10yd/9m worsted weight wool yarn, green pepper color (F)

Approx 20yd/18m worsted weight wool yarn, skewer color (G)

Approx 30yd/27m worsted weight wool yarn, hamburger color (H)

Approx 30yd/27m worsted weight wool yarn, cheese color (J)

Hook: 5.5mm/I-9 or size needed to obtain gauge

Yarn needle

STITCHES USED

Chain (ch)

Double crochet (dc)

Half double crochet (hdc)

Single crochet (sc)

Slip stitch (sl st)

Single crochet decrease (sc2tog)

GAUGE

Take time to check your gauge.

14 sts and 16 rows sc = 4"/10cm

PATTERN NOTES

To change color, work last stitch to where there are 2 loops on hook, yarn over with new color and complete stitch.

GRILL (MAKE 4)

Color Sequence: * 4 rows A, 2 rows B; repeat from *.

With A, ch 11.

Row 1: Sc in 2nd ch from hook and each ch across (10 sc).

Row 2: Ch 6, turn, sc in 2nd ch from hook and next 4 ch, sc in each sc across (15 sc).

Row 3: Repeat Row 2 (20 sc).

Row 4: Ch 5, turn, sc in 2nd ch from hook and next 3 ch, sc in each sc across; change to B in last st (24 sc).

Row 5: Ch 5, turn, sc in 2nd ch from hook and next 3 ch, sc in each sc across (28 sc).

Row 6: Ch 1, turn, 2 sc in first st, sc in next 26 sts, 2 sc in last st; change to A in last st (30 sc).

Row 7: Ch 1, turn, 2 sc in first st, sc across to last st, 2 sc in last st (32 sc).

Row 8: Repeat Row 7 (34 sc)

Row 9: Ch 1, turn, sc in each st across.

Row 10: Repeat Row 7; change to B in last st (36 sc).

Rows 11 and 12: Ch 1, turn, sc in each st across; change to A in last of Row 12.

Row 13: Repeat Row 7 (38 sc).

Rows 14 and 15: Ch 1, turn, sc in each st across.

Row 16: Repeat Row 7; change to B in last st (40 sc).

Rows 17 and 18: Ch 1, turn, sc in each st across; change to A in last st of Row 18.

Row 19: Repeat Row 7 (42 sc).

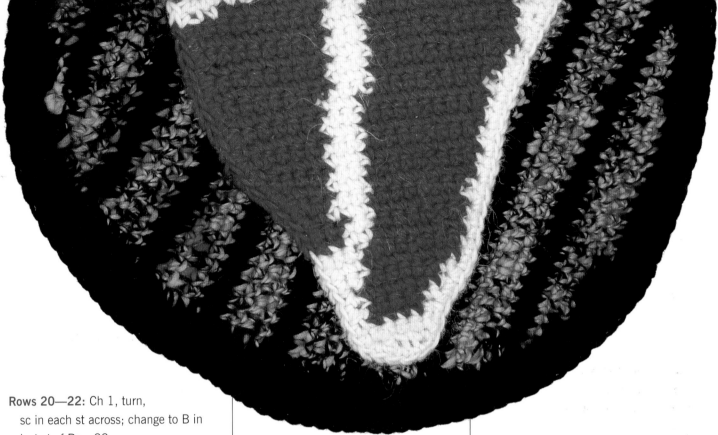

Rows 20—22: Ch 1, turn, sc in each st across; change to B in last st of Row 22.

Rows 23 and 24: Ch 1, turn, sc in each st across; change to A in last st of Row 24.

Rows 25—28: Ch 1, turn, sc in each st across; change to B in last st of Row 28.

Rows 29—33: Repeat Rows 23—27.

Row 34: Ch 1, sc2tog, sc in each st across to last 2 sts, sc2tog; change to B in last st (40 sc).

Rows 35 and 36: Ch 1, turn, sc in each st across; change to A in last st of Row 36.

Row 37: Ch 1, sc2tog, sc in each st across to last 2 sts, sc2tog (38 sc).

Rows 38 and 39: Ch 1, turn, sc in each st across.

Row 40: Ch 1, sc2tog, sc in each st across to last 2 sts, sc2tog; change to B in last st (36 sc).

Rows 41 and 42: Ch 1, turn, sc in each st across; change to A in last st of Row 42.

Row 43: Ch 1, sc2tog, sc in each st across to last 2 sts, sc2tog (34 sc).

Row 44: Ch 1, turn, sc in each st across.

Rows 45 and 46: Ch 1, sc2tog, sc in each st across to last 2 sts, sc2tog; change to B in last st of

Row 46: (30 sc).

Rows 47 and 48: Repeat Rows 43 and 44; change to A in last st of Row 48 (28 sc).

Row 49: Ch 1, turn, sc in first 24 sts; leave remaining sts unworked (24 sc).

Row 50: Ch 1, turn, sc in each st across to last 4 sts; leave remaining sts unworked (20 sc).

Row 51 and 52: Ch 1, turn, sc in each st across to last 5 sts; leave remaining sts unworked; change to B in last st of Row 52. Fasten off A.

Grill Border

With B

Rnd 1: Work 138 sc evenly spaced around outside of grill; join with sl st in first sc.

Rnd 2: Ch 1, * sc in next 18 sts, 2 sc in next st; repeat from * 6 more times; sc in each remaining st around; join with sl st in first sc.

Rnds 3 and 4: Ch 1, sc in each st around; join with sl st in first sc. Fasten off.

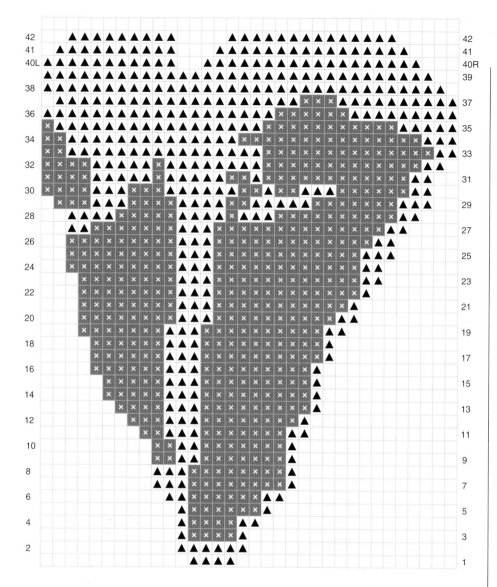

T-BONE STEAK

Note: To reduce the number of yarn ends and to prevent pulls and puckering, carry color that is not in use along the back of the work and weave in with the color in use every 4th st.

Begin Chart

With D, ch 5.

Row 1: Sc in 2nd ch from hook and each ch across (4 sc).

Row 2: Ch 1, turn, 2 sc in first st, sc in next 2 sts, 2 sc in last st (6 sc).

Row 3: Ch 1, turn, sc in first st; with C sc in next 4 sts; with D sc in last st.

Row 4: Ch 1, turn, sc in first st; with C sc in next 4 sts; with D 2 sc in last st.

Row 5: Ch 1, turn, sc in first st; with C sc in next 6 sts; with D sc in last st.

Rows 6—39: Continue in sc, working chart as established.

Left Lobe

Row 40: Ch 1, turn, sc in next 11 sts; leave remaining sts unworked.

Rows 41 and 42: Continue in sc, working chart as established to complete left lobe of steak. Fasten off.

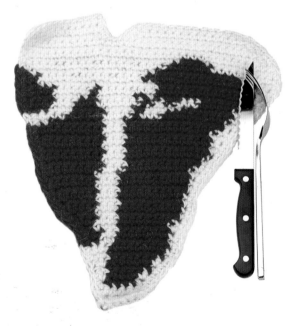

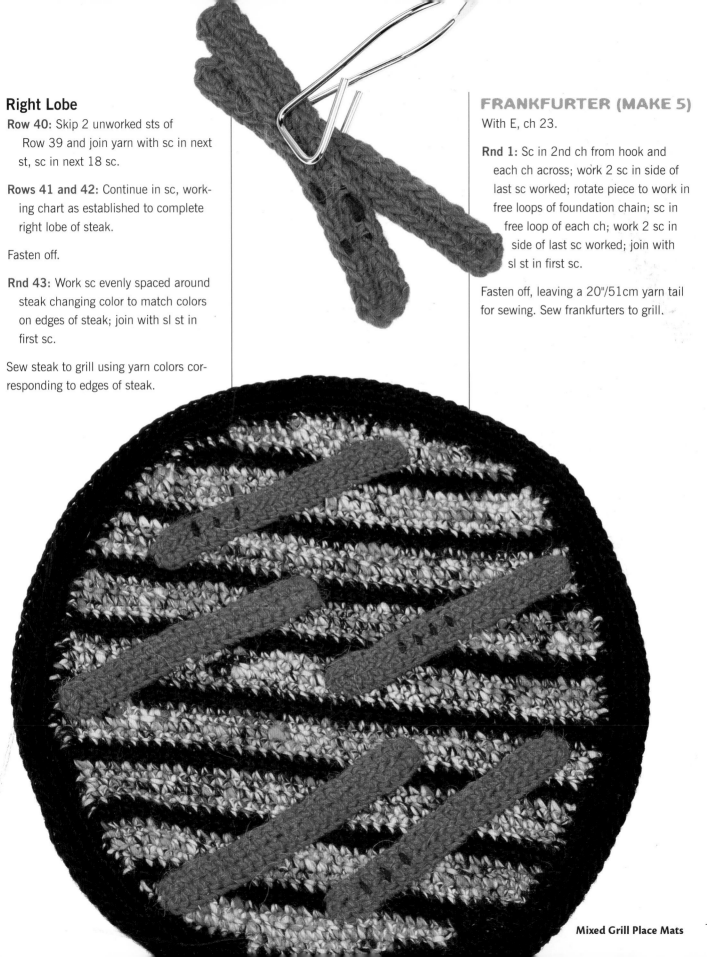

Right Lobe

Row 40: Skip 2 unworked sts of Row 39 and join yarn with sc in next st, sc in next 18 sc.

Rows 41 and 42: Continue in sc, working chart as established to complete right lobe of steak.

Fasten off.

Rnd 43: Work sc evenly spaced around steak changing color to match colors on edges of steak; join with sl st in first sc.

Sew steak to grill using yarn colors corresponding to edges of steak.

FRANKFURTER (MAKE 5)

With E, ch 23.

Rnd 1: Sc in 2nd ch from hook and each ch across; work 2 sc in side of last sc worked; rotate piece to work in free loops of foundation chain; sc in free loop of each ch; work 2 sc in side of last sc worked; join with sl st in first sc.

Fasten off, leaving a 20"/51cm yarn tail for sewing. Sew frankfurters to grill.

KABOBS

Skewer (make 2)

With G, ch 13; join with sl st in first ch to form a ring.

Rnd 1: Ch 1, skip join, (sc in next ch, 2 sc in next ch) 6 times; join with sl st in first sc (18 sc).

Row 2: Ch 39, sc in 2nd ch from hook and each ch across; join with sl st in join of Rnd 1.

Fasten off, leaving a 20"/51cm yarn tail for sewing. Sew skewers to grill.

Tomato (make 2)

With C, ch 2.

Rnd 1: Work 8 sc in 2nd ch from hook; join with sl st in first sc (8 sc).

Rnd 2: Ch 1, 2 sc in each st around; join with sl st in first sc (16 sc).

Rnd 3: Ch 1, (sc in next st, 2 sc in next st) 8 times; join with sl st in first sc (24 sc).

Fasten off, leaving a 20"/51cm yarn tail for sewing. Sew tomatoes to grill over skewers.

Onion (make 2)

With D, ch 5.

Row 1: Sc in 2nd ch from hook and each ch across (4 sc).

Row 2: Ch 1, turn, 2 sc in first sc, sc in next 2 sts, 2 sc in last st (6 sc).

Rows 3—5: Ch 1, turn, sc in each sc across.

Row 6: Ch 1, turn, sc2tog, sc in next 2 sc, sc2tog (4 sc).

Rnd 7: Work sc evenly spaced around edge of onion; join with sl st in first sc.

Fasten off, leaving a 20"/51cm yarn tail for sewing. Sew onions to grill over skewers.

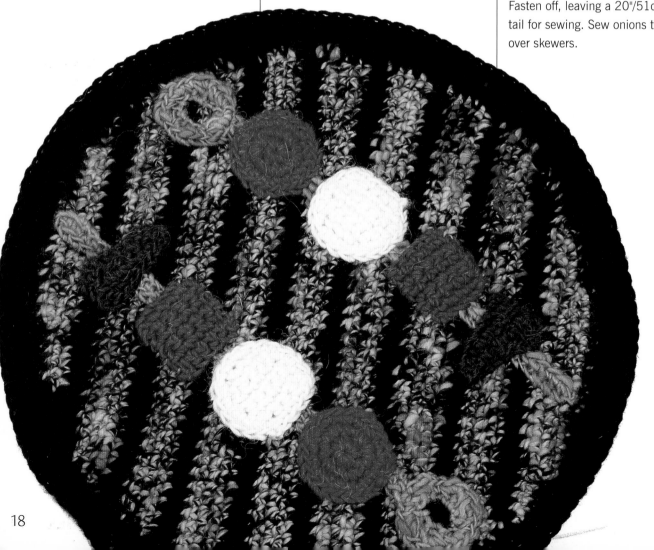

Meat Cube (make 2)

With E, ch 6.

Row 1: Sc in 2nd ch from hook and each ch across (5 sc)

Rows 2—7: Ch 1, turn, sc in each sc across.

Rnd 8: Work sc evenly around edge of meat cube; join with sl st in first sc.

Fasten off, leaving 20"/51cm yarn tail for sewing. Sew meat cubes to grill over skewers.

Green Pepper (make 2)

With F, ch 9.

Row 1: Sl st in 2nd ch from hook and next ch, sc in next 2 ch, hdc in next 2 ch, dc in last 2 ch.

Row 2: Ch 2 (does not count as dc), turn, dc in first 2 sts, hdc in next 2 sts, sc in next 2 sts, sl st in last 2 sl sts. Fasten off, leaving 20"/50cm yarn tail for sewing. Sew green peppers to grill over skewers.

HAMBURGERS

Patties (make 4)

With H, ch 2.

Rnd 1: 8 sc in 2nd ch from hook; join with sl st in first sc (8 sc).

Rnd 2: Ch 1, 2 sc in each st around; join with sl st in first sc (16 sc).

Rnd 3: Ch 1, (sc in next st, 2 sc in next st) 8 times; join with sl st in first sc (24 sc).

Rnd 4: Ch 1, (sc in next 2 sts, 2 sc in next st) 8 times; join with sl st in first sc (32 sc).

Rnd 5: Ch 1, (sc in next 3 sts, 2 sc in next st) 8 times; join with sl st in first sc (40 sc).

Rnd 6: Ch 1, (sc in next 4 sts, 2 sc in next st) 8 times; join with sl st in first sc (48 sc).

Rnd 7: Ch 1, sc in each st around; join with sl st in first sc. Fasten off, leaving 20"/51cm yarn tail for sewing. Sew patties to grill.

Cheese Slice (make 4)

With J, ch 12.

Row 1: Sc in 2nd ch from hook and each ch across (11 sc).

Rows 2—12: Ch 1, turn, sc in each st across.

Fasten off, leaving 20"/50cm yarn tail for sewing. Sew cheese slices to top of patties. Weave in all yarn ends.

This project was created with

3 hanks of Rio De La Plata's Knitting Yarn, 100% Pure New Wool, 3½oz/100g = 140yd/128m, color TS-98 Gold/Orange/Black

3 hanks of Cascade's Pastaza, 50% wool, 50% llama, 3½oz/100g = 132yd/120m, color #008 Black

1 hank of Cascade's Pastaza, 50% wool, 50% llama, 3½oz/100g = 132yd/120m, color #6003 Red

1 hank of Cascade's Pastaza, 50% wool, 50% llama, 3½oz/100g = 132yd/120m, color #001 White

1 hank of Cascade's Pastaza, 50% wool, 50% llama, 3½oz/100g = 132yd/120m, color #010 Rust

1 hank of Cascade's Pastaza, 50% wool, 50% llama, 3½oz/100g = 132yd/120m, color #052 Green

1 hank of Rio De La Plata's Knitting Yarn, 100% Pure New Wool, 3½oz/100g = 109yd/100m, color A-34 Grey

1 hank of Manos del Uruguay, 100% wool, 3½oz/100g = 138yd/126m, color G Dark Brown

1 hank of Manos del Uruguay, 100% wool, 3½oz/100g = 138yd/126m, color W Gold

Hyperbolic Ball

Designer: **Pam Shore**

You don't have to be a math guru, worry about parallel lines, or understand the word "exponential" to appreciate the beauty of these pseudo-spheres. All you need to make this fascinating curiosity are rounds of single crochet. Each round has twice as many single crochet stitches as the previous round until the last round travels a wondrous, twisting path around the sphere.

SKILL LEVEL
Beginner

FINISHED MEASUREMENTS
2" to 7"/5 to 18cm in diameter

YOU WILL NEED (FOR ONE HYPERBOLIC BALL)
Approx 70yd/64m size 10 crochet cotton, OR

Approx 66yd/60m hemp jewelry cord, OR

Approx 92yd/84m plastic canvas yarn, OR

Approx 70yd/64m sport weight yarn, OR

Approx 120yd/110m worsted weight yarn, OR

Approx 171yd/156m super bulky weight yarn, OR

Approx 240yd/220m light worsted weight yarn (2 strands held together), OR

Approx 300yd/275m worsted weight yarn (2 strands held together)

Hook: Select a hook appropriate for chosen thread or yarn that will produce firm stitches. The labels on most thread and yarn packages suggest appropriate hook size; use suggested hook size, or one or two sizes smaller to produce firm stitches.

STITCHES USED
Chain (ch)
Single crochet (sc)
Slip stitch (sl st)

GAUGE
Stitches should be worked to produce a very firm fabric.

PATTERN NOTES
Crochet as tightly as you can without hurting yourself and still being able to insert the hook into the stitches. It can be helpful to slightly stretch the round you are working into.

HYPERBOLIC BALL
Ch 2.

Rnd 1: Working over tail of yarn, work 6 sc in 2nd ch from hook; join with sl st in first sc (6 sc).

Rnd 2: Ch 1, turn, 2 sc in each st around; join with sl st in first sc (12 sc).

Repeat Rnd 2 until ball is of desired size and density.

Last Rnd: Ch 1, turn, sl st in each st around. Fasten off. Weave in end.

This project was created with
1 ball of Coats & Clark's Aunt Lydia's Classic Crochet Thread, size 10, 100% mercerized cotton, 350yd/320m, color #422 Golden Yellow

1 skein of Bernat's Softee Baby,100% acrylic, 5oz/142g = 455yd/416m, color #30205 Pink

1 skein of Uniek's Needleloft Plastic Canvas Yarn, 100% nylon, 2oz/57g = 92yd/84m, color #51002W Christmas Red

1 ball of Lily's Sugar 'n Cream, 100% cotton, 2½oz/71g = 120yd/110m, color #01712 Hot Green

2 balls of Lion Brand's Microspun, 100% microfiber acrylic, 2½oz/70g = 168yd/154m, color #148 Turquoise

1 skein of Caron's Simply Soft, 100% acrylic, 7oz/200g = 366yd/335m, color #9925 Iris

3 balls of Lion Brand's Lion Bouclé, 79% acrylic, 20% mohair, 1% nylon, 2½oz/70g = 57yd/52m, color #208 Parfait

1 ball of The Beadery's Elements, hemp jewelry cord, 100yd/91m, color #1833 Taupe/Beige

1 ball of Darice's Hemp Cord (20lb), 100% hemp, 3½oz/100g = 400ft/122m, Natural

Amigurumi Birds

Designer: **Sharleen Morco**

Whether you use them as tree ornaments or hang them from your rearview mirror, these little guys will fly like Cupid's arrow straight into your heart. Arguably cuter than most puppies, you'll want to crochet up a whole flock of them for yourself and to share.

SKILL LEVEL
Beginner

FINISHED MEASUREMENTS
Height: 3¼"/8.5cm
Diameter: 6"/15cm

YOU WILL NEED (FOR ONE BIRD AND NEST)
Approx 120yd/110m worsted weight yarn, bird color (A)
Approx 47yd/43m bulky weight yarn, nest color (B)
Hooks: 4.25mm/G-6 or size needed to obtain gauge 5.5mm/I-9

STITCH MARKER
Embroidery thread, beak color
Tapestry needle
Two 12mm or 9mm solid black eyes
Polyester fiberfill
About 10"/25.5cm ribbon, ⅛"/3mm wide (optional)

STITCHES USED
Chain (ch)
Single crochet (sc)
Single crochet decrease (sc2tog)

SPECIAL TECHNIQUES
Double ring method (page 121)

GAUGE
Gauge is not crucial
7 sc and 9 rnds = 2"/5cm with smaller hook

PATTERN NOTE
Work progresses in continuous spiral; do not join rounds (unless otherwise instructed). Mark beginning of first round and move marker as each new round is started.

BIRD
Wing (make 2)

With smaller hook and A, form a ring using the double ring method.

Rnd 1: Work 4 sc into ring, tighten ring; do not join; work proceeds in continuous spiral.

Rnd 2: * 2 sc in next st; repeat from * 3 more times (8 sc).

Rnd 3: Sc in each st around.

Rnd 4: Sc in each st around; sl st in next st at end of round to join. Fasten off, leaving a 4"/10cm tail to sew onto body.

Body
With smaller hook and A, form a ring using the double ring method.

Rnd 1: Work 5 sc into ring, tighten ring; do not join; work proceeds in continuous spiral.

Rnd 2: * 2 sc in next st; repeat from * 4 more times (10 sc).

Rnd 3: * Sc in next st, 2 sc in next st; repeat from * 4 more times (15 sc).

Rnd 4: * Sc in next 2 sts, 2 sc in next st; repeat from * 4 more times (20 sc).

Rnds 5—12: Sc in each st around.

Use tapestry needle and embroidery thread to embroider a triangular beak in the center of the body, approx ⅓ down from the top. Attach a 12mm or 9mm solid black eye on either side of the beak. Sew each wing to the side of the body. Begin stuffing with polyester fiberfill.

Rnd 13: * Sc2tog, sc in next 2 sts; repeat from * 4 more times (15 sc).

Rnd 14: * Sc2tog, sc in next st; repeat from * 4 more times (10 sc).

Rnd 15: Sc2tog 5 times (5 sc). Fasten off, leaving a 4"/10cm tail. Use the tapestry needle to weave the tail through last 5 sc. Pull tight to close hole. Weave in end.

Optional: To create a hanging loop, use the tapestry needle to thread the ribbon through the top of the bird's head. Tie ends of ribbon together.

NEST

With larger hook and B, ch 2.

Rnd 1: Work 8 sc in 2nd ch from hook; do not join; work proceeds in continuous spiral.

Rnd 2: * 2 sc in next st, sc in next st; repeat from * 3 more times (12 sc).

Rnd 3: * 2 sc in next st, sc in next 3 sts; repeat from * 2 more times (15 sc).

Rnds 4—6: Sc in each st around.

Rnd 7: Sc in each st around; sl st in next st at end of round to join. Fasten off. Weave in all ends.

This project was created with

1 skein (for each) of Lily's The Original Sugar'n Cream, 100% cotton, worsted weight, 2½oz/70g = approx 120yd/110m, color #00001 White, #00010 Yellow, #01740 Hot Pink, #01742 Hot Blue, #01628 Hot Orange, and #01712 Hot Green

1 skein of Paton's Allure, 100% nylon, bulky weight, 1¾oz/50g = approx 47yd/43m, color #04011

DMC Embroidery Floss, color #975

Bel-Tree Solid Black Eyes: 9mm or 12mm

Catch of the Day

Go fish 'cause you're going to want a whole school of these fanciful potholders and oven mitts. The batik fabric scales are created by working taller double crochet stitches in the front loops of each row.

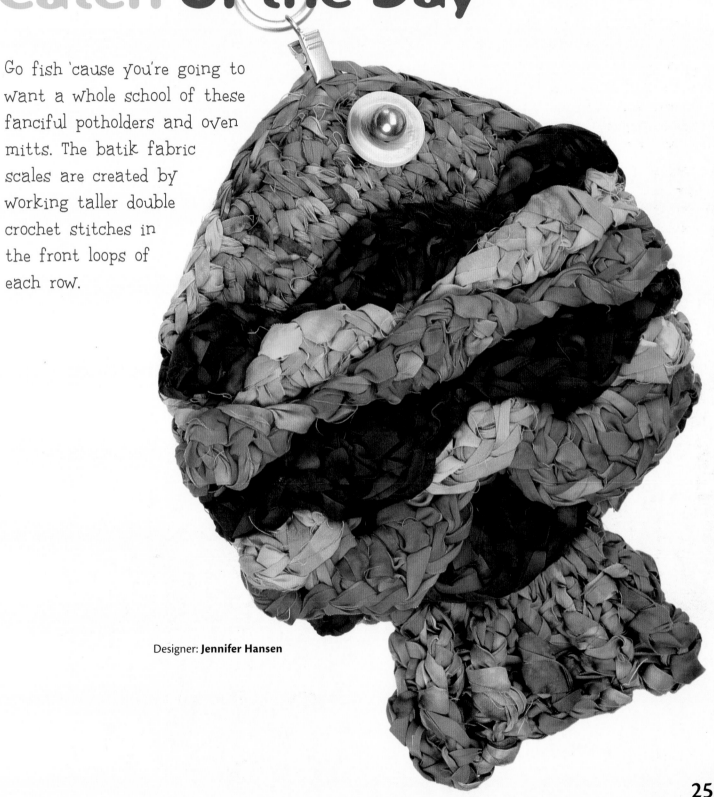

Designer: **Jennifer Hansen**

SKILL LEVEL
Easy/Intermediate

FINISHED MEASUREMENTS
9½" x 7 ½"/24 x 19cm

YOU WILL NEED (FOR ONE POTHOLDER OR OVEN MITT)
Approx 30yd/27m ¾"/2cm cotton ribbon yarn, color of your choice (A)

Approx 30yd/27m ¾"/2cm cotton ribbon yarn, color of your choice (B)

Approx 30yd/27m ¾"/2cm cotton ribbon yarn, color of your choice (C)

Approx 30yd/27m ¾"/2cm cotton ribbon yarn, color of your choice (D)

Hook: 10mm/N-15 or size needed to obtain gauge

½" to 1½"/1.5cm to 4cm button or layered buttons, for eye

STITCHES USED
Chain (ch)

Single crochet (sc)

Slip stitch (sl st)

Shallow single crochet (ssc)

Single crochet decrease (sc2tog)

Shallow single crochet decrease (ssc2tog)

Single crochet double decrease (sc3tog)

Shallow single crochet double decrease (ssc3tog)

Front-post double crochet (FPdc)

Back-post double crochet (BPdc)

GAUGE
Gauge is not crucial.

PATTERN NOTES

Strips cut from cotton fabric, can be substituted for ribbon yarn.

To change color, work last stitch to where there are 2 loops on hook, yarn over with new color to complete stitch.

POTHOLDER
With A, ch 2.

Row 1 (RS): 3 sc in 2nd ch from hook (3 sc).

Rows 2—7: Ch 1, turn, 2 ssc in first st, ssc in each st across, ssc in ch-1 turning ch; change to B in last st of last row (15 ssc).

Row 8: Ch 1, turn, 2 ssc in first st, ssc in each st across, ssc in ch-1 turning ch (17 ssc).

Row 9: Ch 1, turn, working in front loops only, (sc, 3 dc) in first st, skip 3 sts, sc in next st, skip 3 sts, 7 dc in next st, skip 3 sts, sc in next st, skip 3 sts, (3 dc, sc) in last st; change to C in last st.

Row 10: Ch 1, turn, working in front loops only, sc in each st across.

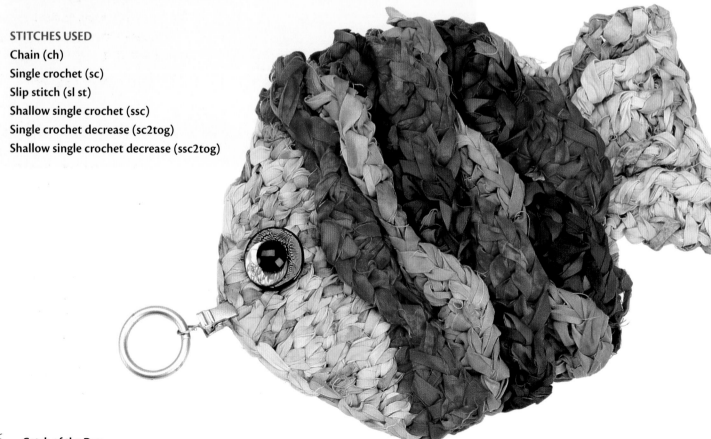

Row 11: Ch 1, turn, working in front loops only, sc in first st, skip 3 sts, 7 dc in next st, skip 3 sts, sc in next st, skip 3 sts, 7 dc in next st, skip 3 sts, sc in last st; change to D in last st.

Row 12: Repeat Row 10.

Row 13: Repeat Row 9; change to B in last st.

Row 14: Repeat Row 10.

Row 15: Repeat Row 11; change to C in last st.

Row 16: Repeat Row 10.

Row 17: Repeat Row 9; change to D in last st.

Row 18: Ch 1, turn, working in front loops only, sc2tog, sc in each st across to last 2 sts, sc2tog (15 sc).

Row 19: Ch 1, turn, working in front loops only, sc2tog, sc in next 2 sts, skip 3 sts, 7 dc in next st, skip 3 sts, sc in next 2 sts, sc2tog; change to A in last st (13 sts).

Row 20: Repeat Row 18 (11 sc).

Row 21: Ch 1, turn, ssc3tog, ssc in each st across to last 3 sts, ssc3tog (7 sts).

Row 22: Ch 1, turn, ssc2tog, ssc in each st across to last 2 sts, ssc2tog (5 sts).

Row 23: Ch 3 (counts as dc), turn, 2 dc in same st, 2 dc in each st across (11 sts).

Row 24: Ch 3, turn, skip first st, (BPdc in next st, FPdc in next st) 5 times.

Row 25: Ch 3, turn, skip first st, (FPdc in next st, FPdc in next st) 5 times.

Fasten off.

Weave in all ends. Sew on button or layered buttons for eye. Stretch tail to widen into fan shape.

OVEN MITT

Front

Leaving a 20"/51cm tail for sewing, work Rows 1—19 of Potholder. Fasten off, leaving another 20"/51cm tail.

Back

With A, ch 2.

Rows 1—8: Work Rows 1-8 of Potholder.

Row 9: Ch 1, turn, working in front loops only, sc in each st across; change to C in last st.

Row 10: Work Row 10 of Potholder.

Row 11: Ch 1, turn, working in front loops only, sc in each st across; change to D in last st.

Rows 12—25: Work Rows 12-25 of Potholder. Fasten off.

Holding wrong sides together, use fabric tails to seam both sides together. Weave in all ends. Sew on button or layered buttons for eye. Weave in all ends. Stretch tail to widen into fan shape.

This project was created with

1 hank each of Princess Mirah Design's Batik Ribbon Yarn, 100% cotton, 1oz/28g = 20yd/18m, lot #CA10-727, CA10-726, CA10-725, CA10-724, HL10-52, LT10-762-C, PW10-825, PW10-830, PW10-834, PW10-831, SW10-805, and YK10-348

Boa Ball Kitty Toy

Designer:
Catherine Peterson

With its tantalizing bobbing action, no cat will be able to resist taking a swipe at this feathery temptation. A boa, elastic, a couple of plastic eyes, and the most basic crochet skills come together in a toy that will turn even your feline friends into crochet enthusiasts.

PUFF

Beginning at "base string" end of boa,
with Q hook, ch 3, sl st in first ch to
form ring.

Rnd 1: Ch 2, work 4 sc in ring; join
    with sl st in top of beginning ch 2.
    Fasten off.

Cut two shapes out of foam or felt to
distinguish eyes. Make a hole for the post
of the plastic eye in each shape.

Pass posts of plastic eyes through foam
or felt shapes, and fasten eyes in two of
the sc.

Fold one end of elastic down about
4"/10cm, forming a loop handle. With
sewing needle and thread, sew in place.

Knot other end of elastic to base string
leading out of the boa at the beginning
ch 3. Thread elastic up through center
of crocheted ring. Pull on elastic so that
knot rests within the crocheted ring, out
of sight.

This project was created with
1 feather boa

Sunnyside Up
Potholder

No chickens were harmed in the design of this potholder. Basic stitches, skillfully arranged, produce a whimsical fried egg that will inspire smiles at any breakfast table.

Designer: **Joy Prescott**

EGG YOLK

Note: Work progresses in continuous spiral; do not join rounds (unless otherwise instructed). Mark beginning of first round and move marker as each new round is started.

Egg Yolk Back

With B, ch 2.

Rnd 1: Work 6 sc in 2nd ch from hook; do not join; work in continuous spiral (6 sc).

Rnd 2: 2 sc in each st around (12 sc).

Rnd 3: (Sc in next st, 2 sc in next st) 6 times (18 sc).

Rnd 4: (Sc in next 2 sts, 2 sc in next st) 6 times (24 sc).

Rnd 5: (Sc in next 3 sts, 2 sc in next st) 6 times (30 sc). Fasten off.

Egg Yolk Front

Repeat Rnds 1—5 of Egg Yolk Back; do not fasten off.

The Egg Yolk Front and Egg Yolk Back are now joined. Before Rnd 6 is complete, stuff yolk lightly with fiberfill.

Rnd 6: Hold wrong sides of Egg Yolk Front and Egg Yolk Back together, and working through both thicknesses, (sc in next 4 sts, 2 sc in next st) 6 times; join with sl st in first sc (36 sc).

Fasten off.

EGG WHITE

Note: Work progresses in concentric rounds; join each round.

Egg White Back

Join A with sl st in back loop only of first stitch in Rnd 6 of Egg Yolk.

Rnd 7: Continuing to work in back loops only, ch 3 (counts as dc here and throughout), dc in next 4 sts, 2 dc in next st, dc in next 3 sts, sl st in next st, dc in next 6 sts, sl st in next st, dc in next st, 2 dc in next st, dc in next 2 sts, 2 dc in next st, dc in next 3 sts, 2 dc in next st, dc in next st, 2 dc in next st, sl st in next st, dc in next 2 sts, (2 dc in next st, dc in next st) twice, 2 dc in last st; join with sl st in top of beginning ch 3 (44 sts).

Rnd 8: Ch 3, dc in next st, (2 dc in next st, dc in next 2 sts) twice, 2 dc in next st, dc in next st, sl st in next st, (dc in next st, 2 dc in next 2 sts) twice, sl st in next st, dc in next st, (2 dc in next st, dc in next 2 sts) 4 times, 2 dc in next st, dc in next st, sl st in next st, dc in next st, (2 dc in next st, dc in next 2 sts) twice, 2 dc in next st, dc in next st, 2 dc in last st; join with sl st in top of beginning ch 3 (60 sts).

Rnd 9: Ch 3, dc in next 2 sts, (2 dc in next st, dc in next 3 sts) twice, 2 dc in next st, dc in next st, sl st in next st, dc in next st, 2 dc in next st, (2 dc in next st, dc in next 3 sts) twice, sl st in next st, dc in next 3 sts, (2 dc in next st, dc in next 3 sts) 3 times, 2 dc in next st, dc in next 2 sts, 2 dc in next st, dc in next st, sl st in next st, dc in next 3 sts, (2 dc in next st) twice, dc in next 3 sts, 2 dc in next st, dc in next 2 sts, sl st in next st, dc in next 2 sts; join with sl st in top of beginning ch 3 (74 sts).

Rnd 10: Ch 3, dc in next 3 sts, (2 dc in next st, dc in next 4 sts) twice, 2 dc in next st, dc in next st, sl st in next st, (dc in next 4 sts, 2 dc in next st) twice, dc in next st, 2 dc in next st, dc in next st, (sl st in next st) twice, hdc in next st, dc in next st, 5 tr in next st, (dc in next 4 sts, 2 dc in next st) twice, hdc in next st, sc in next 10 sts, sl st in next st, sc in next 9 sts, hdc in next st, dc in next st, 5 tr in next st, dc in next st, hdc in next st, sl st in next st, sc in next st, hdc in next st; join with sl st in top of beginning ch-3 (90 sts). Fasten off.

Egg White Front

With right side of Egg White Back facing; join A with sl st in front loop only of first stitch of Rnd 6 of Egg Yolk.

Rnds 7—10: Repeat Rnds 7-10 of Egg White Back; do not fasten off.

Working through both thicknesses of Egg White Back and Egg White Front:

Rnd 11: Ch 1, sc in next 19 sts, sl st in next st, sc in next 17 sts, sl st in next st, sc in next 3 sts, 2 sc in next 3 sts, sc in next 25 sts, sl st in next st, sc in next 12 sts, mark last sc worked, ch 10, sl st in marked sc, ch 1, turn potholder so Back is facing, 15 sc in ch-10 space, sl st again in marked sc, turn potholder so Front is facing, sc in next 5 sts, sl st in next st, sc in next 2 sts; join with sl st in first sc. Fasten off.

This project was created with

1 ball of Lily Sugar 'n Cream, 100% cotton, 2½oz/70g = 120yd/110m, color #01 White

1 ball of Lily Sugar 'n Cream, 100% cotton, 2½oz/70g = 120yd/110m, color #10 Yellow

Fortune Kookies

The fortune reads, "express yourself with yarn," and the cookie is decidedly difficult to chew. But, this is no ordinary fortune cookie. Basic crochet stitches and a healthy sense of humor will have you whipping up batch after batch of these delectable goodies. Hand or machine felting provides the perfect cookie texture and ensures your cookie holds its shape.

Designer: **Donna May**

SKILL LEVEL
Easy

FINISHED MEASUREMENT
Approx 2½"/6.5cm diameter, after felting

YOU WILL NEED (FOR ONE FORTUNE KOOKIE)
Approx 17yd/16m worsted weight 100% felting wool, light gold
Hook: 4.0mm/G-6 or size needed to obtain gauge
Stitch marker
Tape measure
Yarn needle
¾" x 4"/2 x 10cm strip of paper

FELTING SUPPLIES
Cosmetic ball (synthetic, not cotton)
Washing machine
Lingerie bag or pillow protector
Jeans or towels (for added agitation)
Mild detergent

STITCHES USED
Chain (ch)
Single crochet (sc)
Slip stitch (sl st)

GAUGE
Take time to check your gauge.
Cookie circle before felting = 4"/10cm diameter

PATTERN NOTES
Be sure to use 100% wool that is appropriate for felting; do not use super wash.

Cookie is crocheted in continuous spiral; do not join rounds (unless otherwise instructed). Mark beginning of first round and move marker as each new round is started.

You will be crocheting with the wrong side of the cookie facing.

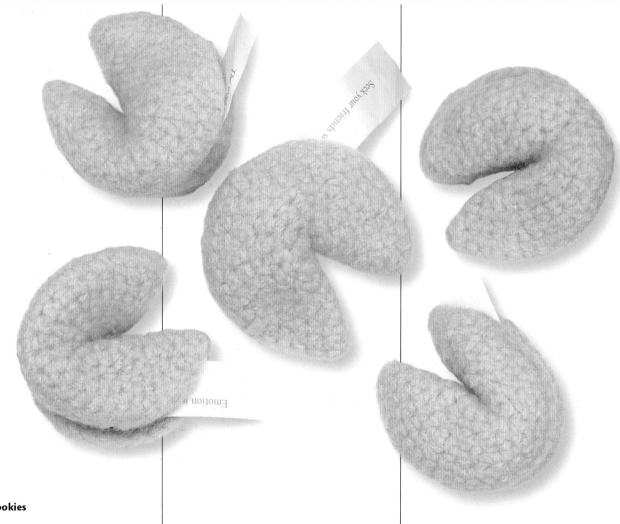

COOKIE

Ch 2.

Rnd 1: Work 6 sc in 2nd ch from hook; do not join; work proceeds in continuous spirals (6 sc).

Rnd 2: 2 sc in each st around (12 sc).

Rnd 3: 2 sc in each st around (24 sc).

Rnd 4: Sc in each st around.

Rnd 5: 2 sc in each st around (48 sc).

Rnd 6: Sc in each st around.

Rnd 7: * Sc in next 3 sts, 2 sc in next st; repeat from * around (60 sc).

Rnd 8: Sc in each st around; sl st in next st at end of round to join.

Remove stitch marker. Fasten off and weave in ends.

Fold Cookie in half and place with flat, folded edge at bottom, curved edge at top. Thread a 10"/25.5cm length of yarn into yarn needle and run through both thicknesses at top center of folded cookie (figure 1); tie a bow. Thread another 10"/25.5cm length of yarn, bring bottom side tips of cookie together and run thread through tips (figure 2); tie a bow to hold tips together.

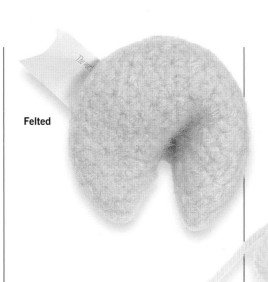

Felted

Unfelted

FELTING

By Hand
(recommended for one cookie)

Using hot water and a generous quantity of mild detergent, vigorously massage cookie to felt. Rinse well with cold water, shape, and air dry.

By Machine
(recommended for several cookies)

Place a cosmetic puff inside each cookie to keep sides separated and help cookie hold its shape. To reduce lint build-up in washer, cookies may be placed inside a large lingerie bag or pillow protector before washing. Place cookies in washer along with a few towels or pairs of jeans. Wash on hot wash cycle with a generous portion of mild detergent. Shape cookie and dry by machine or allow to air dry.

After cookie is dry, untie bows and pull out yarn ties. Remove cosmetic puff. Write message or "fortune" on paper strip and tuck inside cookie.

This project was created with
1 skein of Plymouth Galway, 100% pure wool, 3½oz/100g = 210yd/192m, color #104. Note: 1 skein will make 12 cookies.

Figure 1

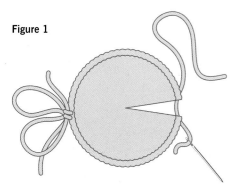

Figure 2

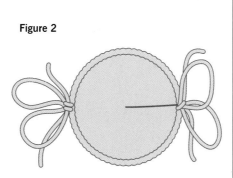

Fuzzy Dice Pillow

Okay, so they're a bit too big to hang on your rearview mirror, and a little awkward for a game of craps, but you can prop your feet up or take a seat on these amusing dice. The pillows are crocheted holding two strands of yarn together and using a large hook and simple crochet stitches.

Designer: **Nanette M. Seale**

36

SKILL LEVEL
Easy

FINISHED MEASUREMENT
12"/30cm cube

YOU WILL NEED (FOR ONE PILLOW)
Approx 450yd/412m bulky weight acrylic yarn, red (A)

Approx 355yd/325m bulky weight eyelash yarn, red (B)

Approx 55yd/50m worsted weight acrylic yarn, black (C)

Hook: 9mm/M-13 or size needed to obtain gauge

Stitch marker

Yarn needle

6 pieces of 2"/5cm thick cushion-type foam, 12"/30.5cm x 12"/30cm square

Craft glue suitable for use with foam

STITCHES USED
Chain (ch)

Single crochet (sc)

Slip stitch (sl st)

SPECIAL TECHNIQUES
Double ring method (page 000)

GAUGE
Take time to check your gauge.

8 sc and 8 rows sc = 4"/10cm

PATTERN NOTES
Glue the pieces of foam together, stacked one on top of the other to form a 12"/30cm x 12"/30cm x 12"/30.5cm cube.

One strand each of A and B are held together throughout.

PILLOW SIDE (MAKE 6)
With one strand each of A and B held together, ch 26.

Row 1: Sc in 2nd ch from hook and in each ch across (25 sc).

Rows 2—25: Ch 1, turn, sc in each st across.

Rnd 26: Ch 1, sc evenly around entire piece, work 3 sc in each corner; join with sl st in first sc. Fasten off.

DOT (MAKE 21)
With C, form a ring using the double ring method.

Rnd 1: Ch 1, work 6 sc in ring, tighten ring; do not join, work proceeds in continuous spiral (6 sc).

Rnd 2: 2 sc in each st around; join with sl st in first st (12 sc). Fasten off, leaving a 10"/25cm tail for sewing.

FINISHING
With yarn needle, sew Dots to Pillow Sides arranging them as for a Die (1 dot on one square, 2 dots on one square, 3 dots on one square, and so on).

Sew Pillow Sides together to form a cube. Place foam cube inside before closing last two edges.

This project (2 Dice) was created with
7 skeins of Lion Brand's Jiffy, 100% acrylic, 3oz/85g = 135yd/124m, color #114 True Red.

11 skeins of Lion Brand's Fun Fur, 100% polyester, 1¾oz/50g = 64yd/59m, color #113 Red.

1 skein Red Heart Super Saver, 100% acrylic, 3oz/85g = 160yd/146m, color #312 Black.

Tadpole Friends

Designer: **Vashti Braha**

These Japanese-inspired crochet companions fit snuggly in the palm of your hand and beg to be squeezed. The delicate look is accomplished with fingering weight yarn and a small hook. Two different stitches can be used: the familiar single crochet or the lesser-known extended single crochet, which creates a subtle starry texture. For further textural variety, consider felting your finished tadpole.

SKILL LEVEL
Easy

FINISHED MEASUREMENTS
Large Tadpole = 2" x 3"/5 x 7.5cm
Small Tadpole = 1½" x 2½"/4 x 6.5cm

YOU WILL NEED (FOR ONE TADPOLE)
Approx 100yd/92m fingering weight
   wool, alpaca, acrylic, or blend, variety
   of tadpole colors
Hook: 3.25mm/D-3 or size needed to
   obtain gauge
Polyester fiberfill
Small yarn needle

STITCHES USED
Chain (ch)
Single crochet (sc)
Slip stitch (sl st)
Extended single crochet (esc)
Extended single crochet decrease
   (esc2tog)

SPECIAL TECHNIQUE
Invisible join (page 122)

GAUGE
Gauge is not crucial.

PATTERN NOTES
Be sure to begin work with a slip knot that can be tightened later. When making the slip knot, use the tail end to create the loop, not the end attached to the ball of yarn. This allows the tail to be tugged to tighten the loop after stitches are worked in the first ch.

Rounds will naturally curve inward, so that wrong side faces out. This helps stitches to be made evenly; do not turn right side out until time to add stuffing.

Tadpoles can be worked in one solid color or in a variety of stripes. Change colors at the end of rounds as desired. See variations at end of instructions for inspiration.

To change color, join round with old color using invisible join. Draw loop of new color through loop on hook. Pull old color to tighten loop.

LARGE TADPOLE
Attach yarn to hook with a slip knot that can be tightened later (see Pattern Notes), ch 2.

Work progresses in joined rounds; do not turn.

Rnd 1: Work 6 sc in 2nd ch from hook; join with invisible join in first sc; tug on yarn tail to close hole in center; work over tail for next few sts of Rnd 2 (6 sc).

Rnd 2: Ch 1, 2 sc in each st around; join with invisible join (12 sc).

Rnd 3: Ch 1, * 2 sc in next st, sc in next st; repeat from * around; join with invisible join (18 sc).

Rnd 4: Ch 1, *sc in next 2 sts, 2 sc in next st; repeat from * around; join with invisible join (24 sc).

Rnd 5: Ch 1, * sc in next 5 sts, 2 sc in next st, (sc in next 7 sts, 2 sc in next st) twice, sc in last 2 sts; join with invisible join (27 sc).

Rnd 6: Ch 1, sc in next 3 sts, 2 sc in next st, (sc in next 8 sts, 2 sc in next st) twice, sc in last 5 sts; join with invisible join (30 sc).

Rnd 7: Ch 1, sc in next 6 sts, 2 sc in next st, (sc in next 9 sts, 2 sc in next st) twice, sc in last 3 sts; join with invisible join (33 sc).

Rnd 8: Ch 1, sc in next 2 sts, (2 sc in next st, sc in next 4 sts) 6 times, sc in last st; join with invisible join (39 sc).

Rnd 9: Ch 1, sc in each st around; join with invisible join.

Embroider face: Thread 18"/45.5cm length of contrasting yarn onto small yarn needle. Fold length of yarn in half to embroider face with double strand.

Rnd 10: Ch 1, sc2tog, (sc in next 4 sts, sc2tog) 5 times, sc in last 7 sts; join with invisible join (33 sc).

Rnd 11: Ch 1, (sc in next 8 sts, sc2tog) 3 times, sc in last 3 sts; join with invisible join (30 sc).

Rnd 12: Ch 1, sc in next 3 sts, sc2tog, (sc in next 8 sts, sc2tog) twice, sc in last 5 sts; join with invisible join (27 sc).

Rnd 13: Ch 1, (sc in next 7 sts, sc2tog) 3 times; join with invisible join (24 sc).

Rnd 14: Ch 1, (sc in next 2 sts, sc2tog) around; join with invisible join (18 sc).

Turn right side out and add stuffing.

Rnd 15: Ch 1, (sc2tog, sc in next st) around; join with invisible join (12 sc).

Rnds 16—21: Ch 1, sc in each st around; join with invisible join.

Add final stuffing.

Rnd 22: * Sl st tightly in back loop only of next st, skip next st; repeat from * 5 more times. Fasten off.

SMALL TADPOLE

Work Rnds 1—7 of Large Tadpole.

Rnd 8: Ch 1, sc in each st around; join with invisible join (33 sc).

Rnds 9 and 10: Work Rnds 11 and 12 of Large Tadpole (27 sc).

Rnd 11: Ch 1, sc2tog, (sc in next 2 sts, sc2tog) 5 times, sc in last 5 sts; join with invisible join (21 sc).

Rnd 12: Ch 1, (sc in next 5 sts, sc2tog) 3 times; join with invisible join (18 sc).

Rnd 13: Ch 1, (sc2tog, sc in next st) around; join with invisible join (12 sc).

Rnd 14: Ch 1, (sc in next 2 sts, sc2tog) around; join with invisible join (9 sc).

Rnds 15—18: Ch 1, sc in each sc around; join with invisible join.

Rnd 19: Sl st tightly in back loop only of next st, *skip next st, sl st tightly in back loop only of next st; repeat from * 3 more times. Fasten off.

Peach-Faced Tadpole

Use peach colored yarn for first 4 or 5 rounds of Small Tadpole, or first 5 or 6 rounds of Large Tadpole. Change to second color for body.

Sporty Stripe Tadpole

Work a round of the tail in a contrasting color, or to set off face from rest of body. To stripe entire body, change color every round. Do not fasten off colors; carry them along the join on the wrong side.

Extended Single Crochet Tadpole

Extended single crochet is a good alternative to single crochet for felting because it is a little less dense. It also has an appealing surface texture.

Ch 3.

Rnd 1: Work 6 extended single crochet (esc) in 3rd ch from hook; join with invisible join (6 esc).

Complete as for Large Tadpole, substituting esc for each sc, and begin each round with ch 2, instead of ch 1. Embroider face after felting.

FELTED TADPOLE

Any tadpole made of 100% felting wool can be felted. Embroider face after felting. Felt tadpole by hand after it is complete. Squeeze and rub tadpole in a small basin of hot soapy water until felted; this may take a little time. Rinse out soap with cold water, squeeze out excess water, and roll in a dry towel to absorb more moisture. Additional drying may be done in clothes dryer on medium heat; check on tadpole every 3 minutes.

This project was created with
1 ball each of Peruvian Collection's Baby Cashmere, 60% alpaca, 30% merino wool, 10% cashmere, 1oz/28g = 109yd/100m, colors #1960 Rose Heather, #2699 Starlight Blue, #3317 Morning Mist, #1742 Dusky Lavender, #3724 Serengeti Sand.

1 ball each of Peruvian Collection's Baby Silk, 80% baby alpaca, 20% silk, 1oz/28g = 109yd/100m, colors #1477 Peridot, #1740 Gentle Violet, #1778 Lotus Blossom, #2124 Oxblood, #2308 Cedar.

Find Your Cocktail Coasters

No more "now which glass is mine?" dilemma. Help guests keep track of their glasses with distinctive and absorbent felted ID coasters. The wool center is a simple spiral of single crochet stitches that is framed with a round of eyelash yarn. When the coaster is felted, the wool center becomes smoother and denser, while the polyester eyelash trim stays fluffy.

Designer: **Deborah Grossman**

SKILL LEVEL
Beginner

FINISHED MEASUREMENTS
6½"/16.5cm diameter of wool center,
before felting

5"/13cm diameter of wool center,
after felting

YOU WILL NEED (FOR ONE COASTER)
Approx 30yd/27m worsted weight felting
wool, coaster color (A)

Approx 6yd/5m eyelash yarn, trim
color (B)

Hook: 5mm/H-8 or size needed to
obtain gauge

Stitch marker

FELTING SUPPLIES
Washing machine (preferably top
loading)

Lingerie bag or pillow protector

Jeans or towels (for added agitation)

Mild detergent

STITCHES USED
Chain (ch)

Single crochet (sc)

Slip stitch (sl st)

GAUGE
Take time to check your gauge.

First 6 rnds = 3"/7.5cm in diameter

PATTERN NOTES
Be sure to use 100% wool that is appropriate for felting; do not use super wash.

Felting time varies according to wool color; darker colors may take less time to felt than lighter colors. Different washing machines also produce different results. Check progress of felting frequently.

Work progresses in continuous spirals; do not join rounds (unless otherwise instructed). Mark the beginning of the first round, and move marker as each new round is started.

COASTER
With A, ch 4; join with sl st to form a ring.

Rnd 1: Work 8 sc in ring; do not join, place marker and work in a spiral.

Rnd 2: 2 sc in each st around (16 sc).

Rnd 3: * Sc in next st, 2 sc in next st; repeat from * 7 more times (24 sc).

Rnd 4: * Sc in next 2 sts, 2 sc in next st; repeat from * 7 more times (32 sc).

Rnd 5: * Sc in next 3 sts, 2 sc in next st; repeat from * 7 more times (40 sc).

Rnd 6: * Sc in next 4 sts, 2 sc in next st; repeat from * 7 more times (48 sc).

Rnd 7: * Sc in next 5 sts, 2 sc in next st; repeat from * 7 more times (56 sc).

Rnd 8: * Sc in next 6 sts, 2 sc in next st; repeat from * 7 more times (64 sc).

Rnd 9: * Sc in next 7 sts, 2 sc in next st; repeat from * 7 more times (72 sc).

Rnd 10: Sl st in first st, sc in same st and in each st around (72 sc).

Sl st in next sc. Fasten off.

From wrong side, join B with sl st in any stitch of Rnd 10.

Unfelted

Rnd 11: Sc in each st around. Form sts over beginning tail of eyelash yarn and ending tail of wool to hide tails. Fasten off. Weave in end.

FELTING

Using washer (preferably top-loading, so you can check on the coasters and stop and start the cycles), set washing temperature on hot (the hottest water yields the best results; turn up water heater, if necessary). Use the least amount of water possible (small load setting, for example). Add a tablespoon of detergent. Place each coaster in a separate zippered pillow protector or lingerie bag, and put them in the washer along with jeans or towels. The jeans and towels help with the agitation and speed up the felting time. Agitate for about 30 minutes (the actual time will vary with each washer). Depending on the length of your wash cycle, you may need to start the cycle over a few times. Don't drain or spin between agitation cycles. Remove from washer when all the stitches have disappeared and the wool feels firm. Rinse with cold water until no soap remains. Roll coasters in a towel to remove excess water. Dry flat (don't use dryer) and smooth fur out from edges of coasters. You can shape the coasters before they dry by pulling around the edges of the wool to even them out.

This project was created with 30yd/27m each of Brown Sheep's Nature Spun, 100% wool, 3½oz/100g = 245yd/224m, colors #144W Limestone, #205 Regal Purple, and #N48 Scarlet.

6yd/5m each of Lion Brand's Fun Fur, 100% polyester, 1¾oz/50g = 64yd/59m, colors #132 Olive, #126 Chocolate, #134 Copper, #112 Raspberry, #109 Sapphire, and #153 Black.

Monster Puppet Pals

Granted they're monsters, and have three or four eyes, but they're also out-and-out lovable. Holding together one strand each of soft acrylic/wool blend and furry eyelash yarn ensures that these monsters are less than scary. Solid or striped rounds of single crochet and a large hook make quick work of this gift for the theatrical youngster in your life, or for yourself.

Designer: **Marty Miller**

FINISHED MEASUREMENTS
Small: 9½"/24cm
Large: 14½"/37cm

YOU WILL NEED (FOR SMALL PUPPET)
Approx 200yd/183m worsted weight
    acrylic/wool yarn, red (A)
Approx 120yd/110m worsted weight
    eyelash yarn, red (B)
Approx 30yd/27m worsted weight
    acrylic/wool yarn, pink (C)

YOU WILL NEED (FOR LARGE PUPPET)
Approx 200yd/183m worsted weight
    acrylic/wool yarn, lime (D)
Approx 120yd/110m worsted weight
    eyelash yarn, lime (E)
Approx 200yd/183m worsted weight
    acrylic/wool yarn, purple (F)
Approx 120yd/110m worsted weight
    eyelash yarn, violet (G)
Approx 30yd/27m worsted weight
    acrylic/wool yarn, red (H)

FOR EACH PUPPET YOU WILL NEED
Approx 10yd/9m worsted weight acrylic/
    wool yarn, white (J)
Approx 1yd/1m worsted weight acrylic/
    wool yarn, black (K)
Hook: 5.5mm/I-9
Yarn needle

STITCHES USED
Chain (ch)
Single crochet (sc)
Slip stitch (sl st)
Loop stitch (lpst)

GAUGE
Gauge is not crucial.

SMALL PUPPET

Mouth Top

With C, ch 7.

Row 1: Sc in 2nd ch from hook and
each ch across (6 sc).

Row 2 (RS): Ch 1, turn, 2 sc in first st,
sc in each st to last st, 2 sc in last st
(8 sc).

Rows 3—4: Repeat Row 2 (12 sc).

Rows 5—14: Ch 1, turn, sc in each sc
across. Fasten off.

Mouth Bottom

Work Rows 1—10 of Mouth Top. Do not
fasten off.

Joining: With right sides of Mouth Top
and Mouth Bottom facing, working
through both thicknesses of last rows, sc
in each sc across. Fasten off.

Eye (make 3)

With J, leaving a 10"/25.5cm tail for
sewing, ch 4.

Rnd 1 (RS): 11 dc in 4th ch from hook;
join with sl st in top of beginning ch.
Fasten off leaving a 10"/25.5cm yarn
tail. Weave yarn tail through back
loop of each dc. Pull tail tight, like a
drawstring, drawing stitches together
with the right sides facing. Bring the
tail through the center, to the other
side; the tops of the stitches form the
top of the eye. Bring a long strand of
K through the bottom of the eye to
the top, and embroider a cross stitch
on the top center. Then bring the yarn
back down to the bottom of the eye.

PATTERN NOTES

The loop stitches are worked from the
wrong side of the fabric; loops form on
the right side. Work the puppet body
with the loops on the outside. After the
Bottom and Top Jaws are joined, the body
is worked in rounds; join, but do not turn
after each round.

Jaw Bottom

With one strand each of A and B held
together, ch 7.

Row 1: Sc in 2nd ch from hook and
each ch across (6 sc).

Row 2: Ch 1, turn, 2 lpst in first st, lpst
in each st across to last st, 2 lpst in
last st (8 lpst).

Row 3: Ch 1, turn, 2 sc in first st, sc in
each st across to last st, 2 sc in last st
(10 sc).

Row 4: Repeat Row 2 (12 lpst).

Row 5: Ch 1, turn, sc in each st across
(12 sc).

Row 6: Ch 1, turn, lpst in each st across.

Rows 7—10: Repeat Rows 5 and 6.
Fasten off.

Jaw Top

Work as for Bottom Jaw through Row
10. Do not fasten off.

Rows 11—14: Repeat Rows 5 and 6.
Do not fasten off.

Body

Rnd 1: Ch 1, turn, sc in each st across Bottom Jaw; sc in first st of Top Jaw, 2 sc in next st, * sc in next st, 2 sc in next st; repeat from * across; join with sl st in first sc (30 sc).

Rnd 2: Ch 1, do not turn, lpst in next 12 sts across Bottom Jaw; lpst in each st across Top Jaw; join with sl st in first st (30 lpst).

Rnd 3: Ch 1, sc in each st around; join with sl st in first st.

Rnd 4: Ch 1, lpst in each st around; join with sl st in first st.

Repeat Rnds 3 and 4 until puppet is 9½"/24cm long. Fasten off.

SMALL PUPPET ASSEMBLY

Attach Eyes

Place two Eyes between Rows 10 and 11 of Top Jaw, and one more Eye above and between the first two eyes. Attach Eyes by bringing the yarn tails through the Body and loosely tying the tails of each Eye together. With one strand of J, sew each Eye to the Body, sewing all the way around; bring the end of J through to the back side and tie it to the other yarn tails. Trim tails, leaving ½"/1.5cm.

Attach Mouth

With the right side of Body facing; join C in corner of Mouth. Working through both thicknesses of Jaws and Mouth, join Mouth to Body by working sc evenly spaced around edges; join with sl st in the first sc. Fasten off. Weave in all ends.

LARGE PUPPET

Mouth

With H, work as for Small Puppet Mouth.

Eye (make 4)

Work as for Small Puppet Eye.

Body

Work as for Small Puppet Body, introducing striping as follows: Begin by holding one strand each of D and E together and work 2 rows of Bottom Jaw. Change to one strand each of F and G, and work the next 2 rows of Bottom Jaw. Continue changing color every 2 rows until Bottom Jaw is complete. Work Top Jaw in same manner. Continue working as for Small Puppet, changing color every 2 rows until puppet measures 14½"/37cm. Fasten off.

LARGE PUPPET ASSEMBLY

Attach Eyes

Place two Eyes between Rows 10 and 11 of Top Jaw, and two more Eyes directly above the first two eyes. Sew Eyes on by bringing the yarn tails through the Body and loosely tying the tails of each Eye together. With one strand of J, sew each Eye to the Body, sewing all the way around; bring the end of J through to the back side and tie it to the other yarn tails. Trim tails, leaving ½"/1.5cm.

Attach Mouth

With the right side of Body facing, join J in corner of Mouth. Working through both thicknesses of Jaws and Mouth, join Mouth to Body by working sc evenly spaced around edges; join with sl st in the first sc. Fasten off. Weave in all ends.

This project was created with

Small Puppet

1 skein of Plymouth Yarn's Encore, 75% acrylic, 25% wool, 3½oz/100g = 200yd/183m, color #1386 Red

2 skeins of Lion Brand's Fun Fur, 100% polyester, 1¾oz/50g = 64yd/59m, color #113 Red

Small amounts each of Plymouth Yarn's Encore, 75% acrylic, 25% wool, 3½oz/100g = 200yd/183m, colors #208 White, #217 Black, and #29 Pink

Large Puppet

1 skein of Plymouth Yarn's Encore, 75% acrylic, 25% wool, 3½oz/100g = 200yd/183m, color #3335 Lime

2 skeins of Lion Brand's Fun Fur, 100% polyester, 1¾oz/50g = 64yd/58m, color #194 Lime

1 skein of Plymouth Yarn's Encore, 75% acrylic, 25% wool, 3½oz/100g = 200yd/183m, color #1384 Purple

2 skeins of Lion Brand's Fun Fur, 100% polyester, 1¾oz/50g = 64yd/59m, color #191 Violet

Small amounts each of Plymouth Yarn's Encore, 75% acrylic, 25% wool, 3½oz/100g = 200yd/183m, colors #208 White, #217 Black, and #1386 Red

Mossy Zen Rock Garden

Random pattern or a very intricate design?
Freeform crochet in delicate, metallic threads mimics
moss on river-smoothed rocks. Scatter a few rocks
on the corner of your worktable or desk to grant you
enlightenment and tranquility. Or arrange them
with a few balls of scrap yarn to make a
zen garden perfect for all your
fiber-related meditations.

Designer: **Gwen Blakley Kinsler**

YOU WILL NEED

Various smooth river rocks

Small quantities of a variety of silk thread, metallic thread, silk cord, fine braid, crochet cotton

Seed beads with holes of an appropriate size for thread

Beading needle

Hook: Appropriate size for selected crochet thread

STITCHES USED

Chain (ch)

Double crochet (dc)

Half double crochet (hdc)

Single crochet (sc)

Slip stitch (sl st)

Treble crochet (tr)

Cluster

Granule stitch

Petal stitch

Popcorn stitch

Shell stitch

Single crochet decrease (sc2tog)

Wave pattern

ZEN ROCK GARDEN COVERS

No river rock is like another. That's one of the reasons you're very unlikely to find detailed instructions for making a crochet lace rock cover. The other reason is that working from detailed instructions is not as fun and liberating as winging it! This project encourages you to realize a personal vision and create unique works of art.

No rules, no counting stitches, no mistakes—this is freeform crochet! Instead, use your imagination, your favorite threads, beads, and stitches to crochet and embellish pieces of crochet lace that approximate the shape of one side of a rock. Make another piece for the other side. Stretch the pieces over the rock and join along the edges using a minimal number of chain and slip stitches, or sew pieces together with needle and thread.

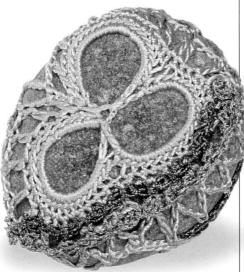

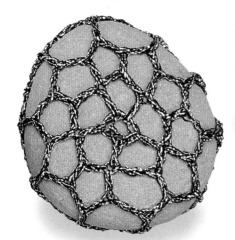

Not sure how to begin? Try any of the following:

- Ch 4, sl st in first ch to form a ring. Work a combination of sc, hdc, dc, and tr in ring to approximate the shape of the rock.

- Make a chain long enough to encircle the rock; join with a sl st. Work more chains and attach them with sl st or sc to encircling chain.

- Ch 4, sl st in first ch to form a ring. (Ch 4, sl st in ring) repeatedly to make a flower shape. In next round work (sc, hdc, dc, hdc, sc) in each ch-4 space.

- Make a small single crochet triangle or square, changing colors each row. At end of last row, do not fasten off; * make a chain long enough to reach next corner of triangle or square with a little slack, sc in next corner; repeat from * around square.

- Start with a tiny granny square or other favorite motif.

- Study nature (e.g., pinecones, flowers, cobwebs) for inspiration.

Not sure how to proceed? Try any of the following:

- Work multiple stitches in a ch space or in the center ch of a length of chain.

- Change color or type of thread.

- Place some beads on the thread and work several stitches in next stitch.

- Work several of your favorite stitches or your favorite stitch pattern.

- Try one of the stitches or stitch patterns described above.

- If you're been working rounds; work in rows. If you're working in rows; work in rounds.

- Make a chain and attach to a random location on the piece.

- Hold two or more threads together and work a few stitches.

Not sure how to finish? Try any of the following:

- Finish before piece becomes bigger than rock. Or, go find a bigger rock.

- Fasten off and attach a different thread on top of stitches already worked. Work some dimensional stitches (e.g. popcorn, granule, bobble). Fasten off again and repeat.

- Work a beaded border.

- Work an uneven border and attach the points of the border to the points of the other side of the rock cover.

- Leave a 1"/2.5cm length of thread when fastening off, and fray the end.

- Study the pictured rocks for inspiration.

This project was created with

Rock 1
(approx 4"/10cm x 2½"/6cm x 1"/2.5cm)

MATERIALS
2 spools of Kreinik's Silk Serica, 3-ply 100% filament silk, 22yd/20m, color #8084

1 spool each of Kreinik's #8 Fine Braid, metallic thread, 11yd/10m, colors #5002, #4001, and #9194

1 spool each of Kreinik's ⅛" Ribbon, metallic ribbon, 11yd/10m, colors #001C and #025

STITCHES
Chain, double crochet, half double crochet, popcorn, shell stitch, single crochet, slip stitch, treble crochet, wave stitch

Rock 2
(approx 2½" x 2" x¼"/6.5 x 5 x 0.6cm)

MATERIALS
2 spools of Kreinik's Silk Serica, 3-ply 100% filament silk, 22yd/20m, color #8086

1 spool each of Kreinik's #8 Fine Braid, metallic thread, 11yd/10m, colors #5002 and #9194.

Green seed beads

STITCHES
Chain, double crochet, half double crochet, popcorn, shell stitch, single crochet, slip stitch

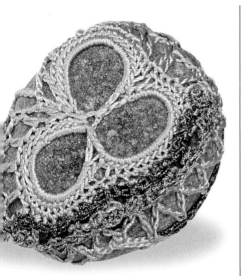

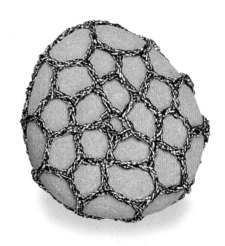

Rock 3
(approx 2¼" x 2¾" x 1"/5.5 x 7 x 2.5cm)

MATERIALS

2 spools of Kreinik's Silk Serica, 3-ply 100% filament silk, 22yd/20m, color #5053

1 spool each of Kreinik's #8 Fine Braid, metallic thread, 11yd/10m, colors #4004 and #088C

STITCHES

Chain, double crochet, granule stitch, half double crochet, single crochet, sl st

Rock 4
(approx 2¼" x 2" x¾"/5.5 x 5 x 2cm)

MATERIALS

2 spools of Kreinik's Silk Serica, 3-ply 100% filament silk, 22yd/20m, color #8084

1 spool of Kreinik's #8 Fine Braid, metallic thread, 11yd/10m, color #5009

STITCHES

Chain, single crochet, slip stitch, petal stitch

Rock 5
(approx 2½" x 2" x¾"/6.5 x 5 x 2cm)

MATERIALS

1 spool each of Kreinik's #8 Fine Braid, metallic thread, 11yd/10m, colors #5010 and #3215

STITCHES

Chain, double crochet, half double crochet, single crochet, slip stitch

Wacky
Wearables

Head to toe funky fashions

Luche Libre
Ski Mask

This ski mask is equally fun to wear during a freestyle wrestling match or while swooshing down the slopes on a snowboard. Practice your crochet color-changing and chart-reading skills while making the perfect gift for the daredevils in your family.

Designer: **Kalpna Kapoor**

SKILL LEVEL
Intermediate

SIZE
This mask will fit most adult heads.

YOU WILL NEED
Approx 150yd/137m light worsted weight yarn, blue
Approx 100yd/92m light worsted weight yarn, yellow
Hook: 4mm/G-6 or size needed to obtain gauge
Stitch markers

STITCHES USED
Chain (ch)
Double crochet (dc)
Half double crochet (hdc)
Single crochet (sc)
Slip stitch (sl st)
Half double crochet decrease (hdc2tog)

GAUGE
Take time to check your gauge.
17 hdc and 14 rows hdc = 4"/10cm

PATTERN NOTES
To change color, work last stitch to where there are 2 loops on hook, yarn over with new color to complete stitch.

MASK

Beginning at top of mask, with A, ch 5; join with sl st in first ch to form a ring.

Rnd 1: Ch 2 (counts as hdc here and throughout), work 6 more hdc in ring; join with sl st in top of beginning ch 2 (7 hdc).

Rnd 2: Ch 2, hdc in same st as join, 2 hdc in each hdc around; join with sl st in top of beginning ch 2 (14 hdc).

Work progresses in continuous spiral; do not join rounds (unless otherwise instructed). Mark beginning of first round and move marker as each new round is started.

Rnd 3: Ch 3, hdc in same st as join, hdc in next st, * 2 hdc in next st, hdc in next st; repeat from * around; do not join (21 hdc).

Rnd 4: * Hdc in next 2 sts, 2 hdc in next st; repeat from * around (28 hdc).

Rnd 5: * Hdc in next 3 sts, 2 hdc in next st; repeat from * around (35 hdc).

Rnd 6: * Hdc in next 4 sts, 2 hdc in next st; repeat from * around (42 hdc).

Rnd 7: * Hdc in next 5 sts, 2 hdc in next st; repeat from * around (49 hdc).

Rnd 8: * Hdc in next 6 sts, 2 hdc in next st; repeat from * around (56 hdc).

Rnd 9: * Hdc in next 7 sts, 2 hdc in next st; repeat from * around (63 hdc).

Rnd 10: * Hdc in next 8 sts, 2 hdc in next st; repeat from * around (70 hdc).

Rnd 11: * Hdc in next 9 sts, 2 hdc in next st; repeat from * around (77 hdc).

Rnds 12—16: Hdc in each st around (77 hdc).

Begin Chart

Rnd 17: Hdc in next 8 sts; with B hdc in next 2 sts; with A hdc in next 19 sts; with B hdc in next 2 sts; with A hdc in next 8 sts; hdc in next 38 sts around back of mask.

Rnd 18: Hdc in next 8 sts; with B hdc in next 3 sts; with A hdc in next 17 sts; with B hdc in next 3 sts; with A hdc in next 8 sts; hdc in next 38 sts around back of mask.

Rnds 19—23: Continue in hdc, working chart as established.

Rnd 24: Hdc in next 6 sts; with B dc in next 6 sts, ch 6, skip next 6 sts (eye made), dc in next 3 sts, ch 6, skip next 6 sts (eye made); with B dc in

next 6 sts; with A hdc in next 6 sts; hdc in next 38 sts around back of mask.

Rnds 25 and 26: Continue in hdc, working chart as established.

Rnd 27: Hdc in next 6 sts; with B hdc in next 13 sts, ch 8, skip 2 sts (nose made), hdc in next 12 sts; with A hdc in next 6 sts; hdc in next 38 sts around back of mask.

Rnd 28: Hdc in next 6 sts; with B hdc in next 13 sts, hdc in each ch, hdc in next 12 sts; with A hdc in next 6 sts; hdc in next 38 sts around back of mask (83 sts).

Rnd 29: Hdc in next 6 sts; with B hdc in next 13 sts, hdc2tog 4 times, hdc in next 13 sts; with A hdc in next 6 sts; hdc in next 38 sts around back of mask (79 sts).

Rnd 30: Hdc in next 6 sts; with B hdc in next 13 sts, hdc2tog 2 times, hdc in next 13 sts; with A hdc in next 6 sts; hdc in next 38 sts around back of mask (77 sts).

Rnd 31: Hdc in next 6 sts; with B dc in next 7 sts, ch 13, skip 13 sts, dc in next 7 sts; with A hdc in next 6 sts; hdc in next 38 sts around back of mask.

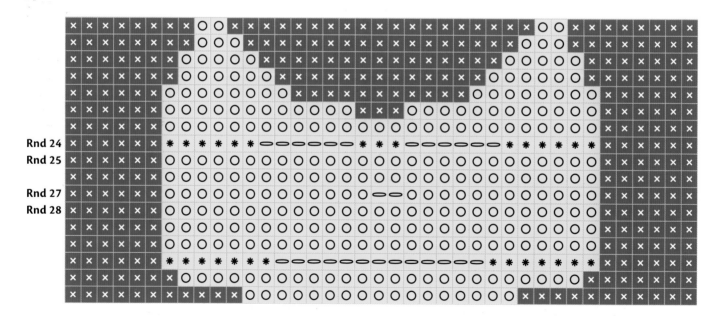

☒	**Yarn A (Blue) hdc**
○	**Yarn B (Yellow) hdc**
✴	**Yarn B (Yellow) dc**
⬯	**Ch-1 & skip 1 stitch with Yarn B (Yellow)**

Rnds 32—33: Continue in hdc, working chart as established.

Rnds 34—36: Hdc in each st around.

Rnds 37—43: Sc in each sc around.

Rnd 44: Sc in each sc around; sl st in next st at end of rnd to join.

This project was created with
1 hank of Classic Elite's Provence, 100% mercerized Egyptian cotton, 3½oz/100g = 205yd/188m, color #2657 De Nimes Blue

1 hank of Classic Elite's Provence, 100% mercerized Egyptian cotton, 3½oz/100g = 205yd/188m, color #2633 Sundrenched Yellow

Medusa Skullie

Even under the threat of turning to stone, folks will not be able to tear their eyes away from this serpent-goddess cap. The cap is crocheted and then ornamented with 21 randomly arranged serpents.

Designer: **Tammy Hildebrand**

SKILL LEVEL
Intermediate

SIZE
This hat will fit most adult heads.

YOU WILL NEED
Approx 480yd/440m worsted weight suede yarn, bright green (A)

Approx 300yd/275m worsted weight metallic suede yarn, green/gold (B)

Approx 5yd/5m worsted weight suede yarn, red (C)

Hook: 3.5mm/E-4 or size needed to obtain gauge

44 peel-and-stick rhinestones

2 silver sequins, 8mm

Approx 3oz/84g unspun wool roving in green

Approx 7yd/6m floral wire, 20-gauge

Hot glue and hot glue gun

Yarn needle

Stitch marker

STITCHES USED
Chain (ch)

Double crochet (dc)

Half-double crochet (hdc)

Single crochet (sc)

Slip stitch (sl st)

Single crochet decrease (sc2tog)

GAUGE
Take time to check your gauge.

16 dc = 4"/10cm

HAT
With A, ch 3; join with sl st in first ch to form a ring.

Rnd 1: Ch 3 (counts as dc here and throughout), work 15 dc in ring; join with sl st in top of beginning ch 3 (16 dc).

Rnd 2: Ch 3, dc in same st as join, dc in next st, (2 dc in next st, dc in next st) 7 times; join with sl st in top of beginning ch 3 (24 dc).

Rnd 3: Ch 3, dc in same st as join, dc in next 2 sts, (2 dc in next st, dc in next 2 sts) 7 times; join with sl st in top of beginning ch 3 (32 dc).

Rnd 4: Ch 3, dc in same st as join, dc in next 3 sts, (2 dc in next st, dc in next 3 sts) 7 times; join with sl st in top of beginning ch 3 (40 dc).

Rnd 5: Ch 3, dc in same st as join, dc in next 4 sts, (2 dc in next st, dc in next 4 sts) 7 times; join with sl st in top of beginning ch 3 (48 dc).

Rnd 6: Ch 3, dc in same st as join, dc in next 5 sts, (2 dc in next st, dc in next 5 sts) 7 times; join with sl st in top of beginning ch 3 (56 dc).

Rnd 7: Ch 3, dc in same st as join, dc in next 6 sts, (2 dc in next st, dc in next 6 sts) 7 times; join with sl st in top of beginning ch-3 (64 dc).

Rnd 8: Ch 3, dc in same st as join, dc in next 7 sts, (2 dc in next st, dc in next 7 sts) 7 times; join with sl st in top of beginning ch 3 (72 dc).

Rnd 9: Ch 3, dc in same st as join, dc in next 8 sts, (2 dc in next st, dc in next 8 sts) 7 times; join with sl st in top of beginning ch 3 (80 dc).

Rnds 10—15: Ch 3, dc in each st around; join with sl st in top of beginning ch-3.

Rnd 16: Ch 1, sc in first st and in each st around; join with sl st in first sc. Fasten off, leaving approximately 30"/76cm yarn tail for sewing Brim to Hat.

LARGE SNAKE FOR BRIM
With B, ch 10; join with sl st in first ch; take care to not twist ch.

Rnd 1: Ch 1, sc in each ch around; do not join; work in continuous spiral (10 sc).

Work progresses in continuous spiral; do not join rounds (unless otherwise instructed). Mark beginning of first round and move marker as each new round is started.

Rnd 2: Ch 1, sc in each st around (10 sc).

Repeat Rnd 2 until snake measures approximately 29½"/75cm. Lightly stuff snake with roving as work progresses. Join with sl st in next st after last round is completed. Insert 2 wire pieces approximately 5"/13cm long to support neck. Do not fasten off.

Top of Head

Row 1: Ch 3, dc in same st as join, 2 dc in next 4 sts; leave remaining sts unworked (10 dc).

Row 2: Ch 3, turn, dc in each st across.

Row 3: Ch 1, turn, skip first st, hdc in next st, dc in next 6 sts, hdc in next st, sl st in last st (2 hdc and 6 dc).

Row 4: Ch 1, turn, sc in first hdc, hdc in next st, dc in next 4 sts, hdc in next st, sc in next st (2 sc, 2 hdc, and 4 dc).

Row 5: Ch 1, turn, sl st across to first dc, ch 1, sc in same st, sc in next st, ch 3, sc in 3rd ch from hook (picot made), sc in next 2 sts (4 sc). Fasten off.

Bottom of Head

Join B with sl st in same st as last st of Row 1 for Top of Head.

Row 1: Ch 3, dc in next 5 sts, dc in same st as first st of Row 1 for Top of Head (7 dc).

Rows 2 and 3: Ch 3, turn, dc in each st across.

Row 4: Ch 1, turn, skip first st, sc in next 5 sts, sl st in last st (5 sc).

Row 5: Ch 1, turn, skip first sc, sc in next 3 sts, sl st in next st (3 sc). Do not turn. Do not fasten off.

Mouth Edging

Working in ends of rows of head and stitches of last rows, slip stitch in each stitch and row around mouth opening. Fasten off.

Tongue

With yarn needle, thread a 4"/10cm length of C tied with large knot in end. Working inside mouth, at back of Row 1 for Bottom of Head, slide needle under sts and hold in place with knot. Slip needle through knot and pull to secure. Trim tongue to desired length. Cut down center of tongue approximately ½"/1cm to create fork.

Eyes

Place one peel-and-stick rhinestone in center of each sequin. Hot glue sequins to Top of Head.

Tail

Working in opposite side of beginning ch of Large Snake; join A with sc in any free loop.

Rnd 1: Ch 1, (sc in next free loop, ch 1) 9 times; join with sl st in first sc (10 sc & 10 ch-1 space). Fasten off.

Rnd 2: Join B with sc in any sc of Rnd 1, skip next ch-1 space, (sc in next st, skip next ch-1 space) 9 times; join with sl st in first sc (10 sc).

Rnds 3—4: Ch 1, sc in each st around; join with sl st in first sc. Fasten off.

Rnd 5: Join A with sc in any sc of Rnd 4, ch 1, (sc in next st, ch 1) 9 times; join with sl st in first sc.

Rnds 6—9: Repeat Rnds 2—5.

Rnds 10—12: Repeat Rnds 2—4. Do not fasten off. Stuff lightly with roving. Insert 2 wire pieces approximately 6"/15cm long to support tail.

Rnd 13: Ch 1, (sc2tog) 5 times; join with sl st in first sc (5 sc).

Rnd 14: Ch 1, sc in each st around; join with sl st in first sc.

Rnd 15: Ch 1, draw up a loop in next 5 sts, yarn over and draw through all loops on hook. Fasten off.

With yarn needle and yarn tail of A from last round of Hat, sew Brim in place around circumference of Hat, leaving approximately 6"/15cm each of Head and Tail free. Shape neck and Tail into desired position, and stitch in place.

SMALL SNAKE (MAKE 11 WITH A)

Ch 8; join with sl st in first ch; take care to not twist ch.

Rnd 1: Ch 1, sc in each ch around; join with sl st in first sc (8 sc).

Rnd 2: Ch 1, sc in each st around (8 sc).

Repeat Rnd 2 until snake measures desired length, making snakes of various lengths. Join with sl st in next st after last round is completed. Do not fasten off.

Top of Head

Row 1: Ch 1, draw up loop in next 4 sts, yarn over and pull through all loops on hook, leave remaining sts unworked.

Row 2: Ch 1, do not turn, (sc, 7 dc, sc) in back bar of ch-1 just made (first ch from hook). Do not turn or fasten off.

Bottom of Head

Worked in remaining unworked sts of top of body of snake.

Row 1: Draw up a loop in next 4 sts, yarn over and draw through all loops on hook.

Row 2: Ch 1, do not turn, (sc, 5 dc, sc) in back bar of ch 1 just made (first ch from hook), sl st in beginning of Row 1 on Top of Head to shape mouth. Fasten off.

Lightly stuff with roving. Insert 2 lengths of wire for support.

Tongue

Work as for Large Snake Tongue.

Eyes

Place 2 peel-and-stick rhinestones on Top of Head.

SMALL METALLIC SNAKE (MAKE 10 WITH B)

Ch 10; join with sl st in first ch; take care to not twist ch.

Rnd 1: Ch 1, sc in each ch around; join with sl st in first sc (10 sc).

Rnd 2: Ch 1, sc in each st around (10 sc).

Repeat Rnd 2 until snake measures desired length, making snakes of various lengths. Join with sl st in next st after last round is completed. Do not fasten off.

Top of Head

Row 1: Ch 1, draw up loop in next 5 sts, yarn over and pull through all loops on hook, leave remaining sts unworked.

Row 2: Ch 1, do not turn, (sc, 7 dc, sc) in back bar of ch 1 just made (first ch from hook). Do not turn or fasten off.

Bottom of Head

Worked in remaining unworked sts of top of body of snake.

Row 1: Draw up a loop in next 5 sts, yarn over and draw through all loops on hook.

Row 2: Ch 1, do not turn, (sc, 5 dc, sc) in back bar of ch 1 just made (first ch from hook), sl st in beginning of Row 1 on Top of Head to shape mouth. Fasten off.

Lightly stuff with roving. Insert 2 lengths of wire for support.

Tongue

Work as for Large Snake Tongue.

Eyes

Place 2 peel-and-stick rhine-stones on Top of Head.

FINISHING

Using yarn needle, sew small snakes in random locations on top of Hat.

This project was created with

4 balls of Berroco Suede, 100% nylon, 1.75oz/50g = 120yd/111m, color #3786 Aloe Vera

3 balls of Berroco Suede Deluxe, 85% nylon,10% rayon, 5% polyester, 1.75oz/50g = 100yd/92m, color #3920 Tonto Gold

1 ball of Berroco Suede, 100% nylon, 1.75oz/50g = 120yd/111m, color #3752 Renegade Red

Sulyn peel & stick rhinestones

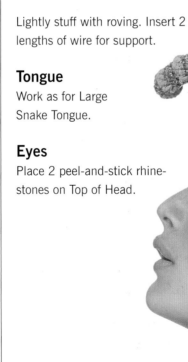

Diva Flip-Flops

Designer: **Kim Lewis**

Be sure to get a pedicure when you wear these thongs, because your feet will definitely draw attention. Add a little podiatric drama to casual flip-flops with novelty yarn and felted wool embellishments. Eyelash yarn is firmly attached to the flip-flop straps with single crochet stitches worked around each strap. A fun and easy first project for a new crocheter.

SKILL LEVEL
Beginner

YOU WILL NEED (FOR ONE PAIR OF FLIP-FLOPS)
Approx 60yd/55m eyelash yarn, color of
   your choice (A)
Approx 20yd/18m worsted weight
   felting wool (optional, for skulls),
   off-white (B)
Hooks: 5mm/H-8
   5.5mm/I-9

PAIR OF FLIP FLOPS
Embroidery thread (optional, for
   skulls), black
Embroidery needle (optional, for skulls)
Yarn needle
Hot glue gun and glue sticks, or
   fabric glue
Felting Supplies (optional, for skulls)
Washing machine (preferably
   top loading)
Lingerie bag or pillow protector
Jeans or towels (for added agitation)
Mild detergent

STITCHES USED
Slip stitch (sl st)
Single crochet (sc)

FLIP-FLOP TRIM
With A, make slip knot.

Hold flip-flop with toe facing and insert larger hook, from right to left, under top of left strap. Bring yarn with slip knot in from the left and put yarn on hook. Pull the hook back until your right hand, holding the hook, is on the right side of the strap and your left hand, holding the working yarn, is on the left side of the strap. Bring crochet hook OVER the strap, yarn over, and draw through loop on hook (slip stitch made).

Insert hook under the strap again, yarn over, and draw yarn back to right side of strap (2 loops on hook). Bring cro- chet hook over the strap, yarn over, and draw through both loops on hook (single crochet made). Continue working single crochet in this manner until work reaches the toe strap. Pause every few stitches and slide the stitches together to thoroughly cover the straps and make the fur dense and fluffy. Work in the same manner around the toe strap and down the right strap. After you cover the toe strap and begin the opposite foot strap, the heel of the flip-flop should be facing you.

Fasten off. With yarn needle, weave in all ends.

SKULLS
(MAKE 2 — OPTIONAL)

PATTERN NOTE

Be sure to use 100% wool that is appropriate for felting; do not use super wash.

With B and smaller hook, ch 26.

Row 1: Sc in 2nd ch from hook and each ch across (25 sc).

Rows 2—10: Ch 1, turn, sc in each st across. Fasten off.

Weave in all ends.

Felting

Using washer (preferably top-loading, so you can check on the felting and stop and start the cycles), set washing temperature on hot (the hottest water yields the best results; turn up water heater, if necessary). Use the least amount of water possible (small load setting, for example). Add a tablespoon of detergent. Place wool square in a zippered pillow protector or lingerie bag, and put them in the washer along with jeans or towels. The jeans and towels help with the agitation and speed up the felting time. Agitate for about 30 minutes (the actual time will vary with each washer). Depending on the length of your wash cycle, you may need to start the cycle over a few times. Don't drain or spin between agitation cycles. Remove from washer when all the stitches have disappeared and the wool feels firm. Rinse with cold water until no soap remains. Roll wool square in a towel to remove excess water. Press square flat, and allow to air dry completely before cutting.

Using project photo for reference, cut two skull shapes from felted wool square. Use embroidery thread and needle to stitch eye and teeth details on the skulls. Glue or sew one skull to each flip-flop near the top of the toe strap. Let glue dry completely before wearing.

This project was created with

1 ball of Lion Brand's Fun Fur, 100% polyester, 1½oz/40g = 57yd/52m, color #143 Black

1 ball of Knit Pick's Wool of the Andes, 100% wool, 1¾oz/50g = 110yd/100m, color #23432 Cloud

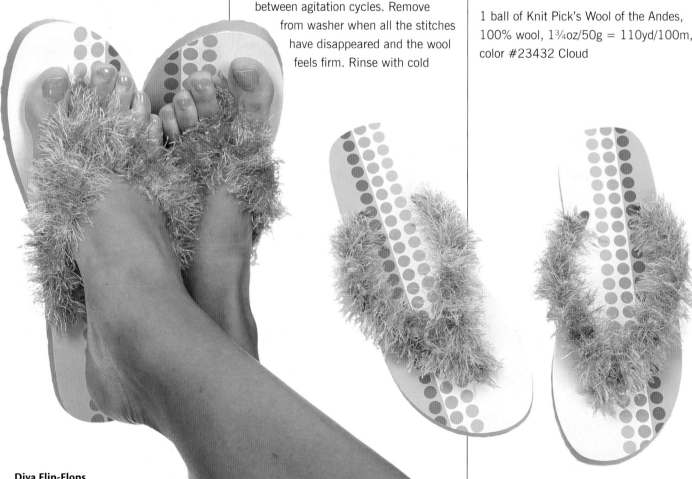

Eve's
Fig Leaf Halter

Eve never had it so good. Soft cotton fig leaves offer a major improvement over the scratchy and short-lived originals. The stylish, skirted halter with a tongue-in-cheek twist is cleverly constructed with basic crochet and post stitches.

Designer: **Joy Prescott**

SKILL LEVEL
Intermediate

SIZE
One size fits bust sizes 33—38 A—C cups.

YOU WILL NEED
Approx 450yd/411m Size #3 crochet
   cotton, halter color (A)
Approx 150yd/137m Size #3 crochet
   cotton, fig leaf color (B)
Hook: 3.5mm/E-4 or size needed to
   obtain gauge

STITCHES USED
Chain (ch)
Double crochet (dc)
Half double crochet (hdc)
Single crochet (sc)
Slip stitch (sl st)
Treble crochet (tr)
Back-post double crochet (BPdc)
Double crochet decrease (dc2tog)
Front-post double crochet (FPdc)
Single crochet decrease (sc2tog)

GAUGE
Take time to check your gauge.
16 sts and 18 rows sc = 4"/10cm

CUPS
With A, ch 112.

Base Row

Row 1 (Front): Sc in 2nd ch from hook
and in each ch across (111 sc).

LEFT CUP
Row 2: Ch 1, turn, sc2tog, sc in next
51 sts, sc2tog; leave remaining sts
unworked (53 sc).

Row 3: Ch 1, turn, sc2tog, sc in each st
across to last 2 sts, sc2tog (51 sc).

Row 4: Ch 1, turn, sc in each sc across.

Rows 5-50: Repeat Rows 3 and 4 (5
sc). Do not fasten off.

SHOULDER STRAP
Rows 51-135: Ch 1, turn, sc in each st
across (5 sc). Fasten off.

RIGHT CUP
Skip one unworked st of Row 1 (Center
of Halter). Join A with sl st in next unworked st of Row 1.

Row 2: Ch 1, inserting hook in same
st as join sc2tog, sc in next 51 sts,
sc2tog (53 sc).

Rows 3—50: Work Rows 3—50 of
Left Cup.

Rows 51—135: Work Rows 51—135 of
Shoulder Strap. Fasten off.

MIDRIFF
Working in opposite side of foundation
chain, join A with sl st in first st.

Row 1: Ch 3 (counts as dc here and
   throughout), dc in each st across
   (111 dc).

Row 2: Ch 3, turn, dc in next 4 sts,
   * BPdc in next st, dc in next 5 sts;
   repeat from * across.

Row 3: Ch 3, turn, dc in next 4 sts,
   * FPdc in next st, dc in next 5 sts;
   repeat from * across.

Rows 4—15: Repeat Rows 2 and 3.
Fasten off.

FINISHING

Side Tie
With Front of Halter facing, and working
along left side of Halter; join A with sl st
in side of Row 2 of Midriff.

Row 1: Ch 1, sc in same place as join,
   work 4 sc evenly spaced in ends of
   rows (5 sc).

Rows 2-100: Ch 1, turn, sc in each st
   across. Fasten off.

With Back of Halter facing, and working
along right side of Halter, repeat Side Tie
on other side of Halter.

Center Front Trim
With Front of Halter facing, join A with sl
st in side of 2nd Row of Left Shoulder Tie
(2 rows above last row of Left Cup).

Row 1: Ch 1, sc in side of next row,
   hdc in side of next row, * dc in side of
   next 2 rows, dc2tog in side of next 2
   rows*, repeat from * to * to within 1
   st of Center Halter, dc3tog; repeat from

* to * up other side of Halter to Right Shoulder Strap, hdc in side of next row, sc in side of next row.

Row 2: Ch 1, turn, skip first st, sc in next 2 sts, hdc in next st, *dc in next 2 sts, dc2tog*; repeat from * to * to within 1 st of Halter Center, dc3tog; repeat from * to * to last 2 sts, hdc in next st, sc in next st, sl st in next st. Fasten off.

Edging

With Front facing, join A with sl st in lower left corner of Midriff.

Row 1: Ch 1, work sc evenly spaced across ends of Midriff and Left Side Tie rows; 3 sc in corner of Left Side Tie, sc across end of Tie, 3 sc in next corner of Left Side Tie, sc in ends of Left Side Tie rows; working in ends of rows, * sc in next 2 rows, sc2tog; repeat from * across to Left Shoulder Tie; sc in ends of rows of Left Shoulder Tie, 3 sc in corner of Left Shoulder Tie, sc across end of Tie, 3 sc in next corner of Left Shoulder Tie, sc in ends of Left Shoulder Tie rows; sc in each st across Center Front Trim to center 3 sts, sc3tog, sc in each st across Center Front Trim to Right Shoulder Tie. Continue working sc around Ties and side of Midriff as established to lower right corner of Midriff. Fasten off. Weave in ends.

FIG LEAF (MAKE 2)

First Half

With B, ch 33.

Row 1: Sc in 2nd ch from hook and in each ch across (32 sc).

Row 2: Ch 1, turn, 2 sc in first st, sc in each st across to last 2 sts, sc2tog.

Row 3: Ch 1, turn, sc2tog, sc in each st across to last 2 sts, 2 sc in last st.

Row 4: Ch 1, turn, sc in each st across to last 2 sts, sc2tog (31 sc).

Row 5: Ch 1, turn, sc2tog, sc in each st across to last st, 2 sc in last st.

Row 6: Ch 1, turn, 2 sc in first sc, sc in next 14 sts; leave remaining sts unworked (16 sc).

Row 7: Ch 1, turn, 2 sc in first st, sc in each st across to last st, 2 sc in last st (18 sc).

Row 8: Ch 1, turn, 2 sc in first st, sc in each st across to last st, 2 sc in last st (20 sc).

Row 9: Ch 1, turn, 2 sc in first st, sc in each st across (21 sc).

Row 10: Repeat Row 8 (23 sc).

Row 11: Ch 1, turn, 3 sc in first st, sc in each st across (25 sc).

Row 12: Ch 1, turn, sc in each sc across to last st, 2 sc in last st (26 sc).

Row 13: Ch 1, turn, 2 sc in first st, sc in each st across to last 2 sts, sc2tog.

Row 14: Repeat Row 12 (27 sc).

Row 15: Repeat Row 13.

Row 16: Ch 1, turn, sc in each st across.

Row 17: Ch 1, turn, 2 sc in first st, sc in next 14 sts; leave remaining sts unworked (16 sc).

Row 18: Ch 1, turn, sc2tog, sc in each st across to last st, 2 sc in last st.

Rows 19-21: Repeat Row 16.

Row 22: Ch 1, turn, sc2tog, sc in each st across (15 sts).

Row 23: Ch 1, turn, sc in each st across to last 2 sts, sc2tog (14 sc).

Row 24: Ch 1, turn, skip first st, sl st in next 3 sts, sc in next 5 sts, sl st in next st. Fasten off.

Working in unworked sts of Row 16, skip one st; join with sl st in next st.

Row 18: Ch 1, sc in same st and in each st across (11 sc).

Row 19: Ch 1, turn, sc2tog, sc in each st across (10 sc).

Row 20: Ch 1, turn, sc in each st across to last 2 sts, sc2tog (9 sc).

Row 21: Ch 1, turn, sc2tog twice, sc in next 4 sts, 2 sc in last st (8 sc).

Row 22: Ch 1, turn, sc in each st across to last 2 sts, sc2tog (7 sc).

Row 23: Ch 1, turn, sc2tog, sc in next 3 sts, sc2tog (5 sc).

Row 24: Ch 1, turn, sc2tog, sc in next st, sl st in next st. Fasten off.

Working in unworked sts of Row 5, skip 2 sts; join with sl st in next st.

Row 6: Ch 1, sc in each st across (14 sc).

Row 7: Ch 1, turn, sc in each st across to last 2 sts, sc2tog (13 sc).

Row 8: Ch 1, turn, sc2tog, sc in each st across to last 2 sts, sc2tog (11 sc).

Row 9: Ch 1, turn, sc2tog, sc in next 5 sts, sc2tog twice (8 sc).

Row 10: Ch 1, turn, sc2tog, sc in next 4 sts, sc2tog (6 sc).

Second Half

With wrong side of Row 1 of First Half facing, sl st in first st on opposite side of foundation chain.

Row 1: Ch 1, sc in same st and each st across.

Repeat all rows beginning at Row 2 of First Half.

FINISHING

Join with sl st at stem end of leaf.

Rnd 1: Ch 1, work sc evenly spaced around leaf.

Fasten off, leaving a 12"/30.5cm yarn tail for sewing. Position fig leaf on Halter Cup and sew in place.

This project was created with
3 balls of DMC's Senso, 100% cotton, 1¾oz/50g = 150yd/137m, color #1002

1 ball of DMC's Senso, 100% cotton, 1¾oz/50g = 150yd/ 137m, color #1009

Haute Hardware
Leg Warmers & Glovelets

Some crochet aficionados see yarn and beads everywhere; even in the hardware store. Sturdy mason twine and toothed washers have never been put to more creative use. Colorful rounds of single crochet, post stitches, and washer "bling" form the most durable leg warmers and glovelets you'll ever own.

Designer: **Drew Emborsky**

SKILL LEVEL
Easy

FINISHED MEASUREMENTS
One size fits most adults

FOR ONE PAIR OF GLOVELETS
YOU WILL NEED
Approx 75yd/69m mason twine, lime green (A)

Approx 75yd/69m mason twine, hot pink (B)

Approx 75yd/69m mason twine, white (C)

FOR ONE PAIR OF LEG WARMERS
YOU WILL NEED
Approx 300yd/275m mason twine, lime green (A)

Approx 300yd/275m mason twine, hot pink (B)

Approx 300yd/275m mason twine, white (C)

Hook: 5mm/H-8 or size needed to obtain gauge

24 exterior-tooth lock washers, 5/6"/20mm

36 exterior-tooth lock washers, 3/8"/10mm

12 exterior-tooth lock washers, ¼"/6mm

24 exterior-tooth lock washers, #10

24 exterior-tooth lock washers, #8

STITCHES USED
Chain (ch)

Single crochet (sc)

Slip stitch (sl st)

Back-post double crochet (BPdc)

Front-post double crochet (FPdc)

GAUGE
Take time to check your gauge.

16 sts and 4 rows sc = 4"/10cm

PATTERN NOTES

Work progresses in continuous spiral; do not join rounds (unless otherwise instructed). Mark beginning of first round and move marker as each new round is started.

To provide a little stretch, all single crochet are worked in the back loops only.

To add a lock washer, pull washer up close to stitch just completed, work single crochet in next stitch. Tug gently on washer to pull into place.

To change color, work last stitch to where there are 2 loops on hook, yarn over with new color to complete stitch.

LEG WARMER (MAKE 2)
Thread twelve ⅝"/20mm washers onto B, twelve ⅝"/20mm washers onto C, and twelve ⅜"/10mm washers onto A.

With A, ch 38; join with sl st in first ch to form a ring, take care to not twist chain.

Rnd 1: Ch 1, sc in each ch around; do not join; work in continuous spiral (48 sc).

Work all single crochet in back loops only.

Rnd 2: Sc in each st around; change to B in last st.

Rnd 3: Sc in each st around.

Rnd 4: * Sc in next 8 sts, add washer; repeat from * around (8 washers added).

Rnd 5: Sc in each st around.

Rnd 6: Sc in first 3 sts, add washer, *sc in next 8 sts, add washer; repeat from * around; sc in last 5 sts.

Rnd 7: Sc in each st around; change to C in last st.

Rnds 8—12: Repeat Rnds 3—7; change to A in last st of Rnd 12.

Rnds 13-16: Repeat Rnds 3—6.

Before changing to B in last stitch of Rnd 17, thread twelve ⅜"/10mm washers onto B, twelve #10 washers onto C, and twelve #10 washers on A.

Rnd 17: Sc in each st around; change to B in last st.

Rnd 18-31: Repeat Rnds 3—16.

Before changing to B in last stitch of Rnd 31, thread twelve #8 washers onto B and twelve #8 washers onto C.

Rnd 32: Sc in each st around; change to B in last st.

Rnds 33-42: Repeat Rnds 3—12; change to B in last st of Rnd 42.

Rnd 43: Dc in each st and ch around (48 dc).

Rnds 44 and 45: * BPdc in next st, FPdc in next st; repeat from * around; join with sl st in top of first BPdc.

Fasten off. Weave in all ends.

GLOVELET (MAKE 2)

Thread twelve 3/8"/10mm washers onto B, and twelve ¼"/6mm washers onto C.

With A, ch 36; join with sl st in first ch to form a ring, take care to not twist chain.

Rnd 1: Ch 1, sc in each ch around; do not join, work in a continuous spiral (36 sc).

Work all single crochet in back loops only.

Rnd 2: Sc in each st around; change to B in last st.

Rnd 3: Sc in each st around.

Rnd 4: * Sc in next 6 sts, add washer; repeat from * around (6 washers added).

Rnd 5: Sc in each st around.

Rnd 6: Sc in first 2 sts, add washer, * sc in next 6 sts, add washer; repeat from * around; sc in last 4 sts.

Rnd 7: Sc in each st around; change to C in last st.

Rnds 8—12: Repeat Rnds 3—7; change to A in last st of Rnd 12.

Create Thumbhole

Rnd 13: Sc in next 3 sts, ch 6, skip 10 sts, sc in next 23 sts.

Rnd 14: Dc in each st and ch around (32 dc).

Rnd 15: * BPdc in next st, FPdc in next st; repeat from * around; join with sl st in top of first BPdc.

Fasten off. Weave in all ends.

This project was created with
5 cones each of Everbilt's Mason Twine, 100% nylon, 7oz/200g = 75yd/69m, colors Lime Green, Hot Pink, and White.

Bunches of Blobble Belts

Round, pliable, vinyl yarn makes for mod, bright belts with moderate stretch. A basic belt pattern is enhanced with three style variations: fringed, sequined, and "bling". Wear your jelly belt with a bikini, capri pants, as a sunhat band, or as a skinny scarf.

Designer: **Vashti Braha**

SKILL LEVEL
Easy

FINISHED MEASUREMENT
Length: 43"/109cm – 60"/152cm

YOU WILL NEED (FOR ONE BELT)
Approx 60yd/55m bulky weight clear vinyl yarn for each belt, color of your choice

Hooks: 9mm/M-13 or size needed to obtain gauge

10mm/N-15 or size needed to obtain gauge (for sequined belt only)

Approx 60yd/54m sequined carry-along thread (for sequined belt only)

Protectant wipes for vinyl

2 jumbo drop-style clear acrylic crystal beads with large holes (for bling belt only)

3 large round clear acrylic crystal beads with large holes (for bling belt only)

Clear glue

STITCHES USED
Chain (ch)
Double crochet (dc)
Half-double crochet (hdc)
Single crochet (sc)
Slip stitch (sl st)
Cluster (CL)

GAUGE
Take time to check your gauge.
4 rows (2 clusters) = 3"/7.5cm with smaller hook

PATTERN NOTES
Wipe the hook with protectant wipes made for vinyl before starting to crochet and before starting each Cluster.

Tie all knots very tightly, stretching the yarn, to ensure permanence of knot.

Jelly yarn may show bumps from being wound into skeins. Hang finished belt over a chair for a day; all stitches will then appear more regular and the blobbles will stand out.

For best results always turn in the same direction at ends of rows (clockwise for right-handers, counter-clockwise for left-handers).

BASIC BELT

Leaving a 16"/40.5cm yarn tail, place yarn on hook with a slip knot that is secured with a tight knot; ch 4.

Row 1: CL in 3rd ch from hook, hdc in last ch.

Row 2: Turn, ch 4, skip first st, skip CL, dc in top of beginnning ch.

Row 3: Turn, ch 2, CL in ch-4 space, hdc in 3rd ch of ch-4 turning ch.

Row 4: Turn, ch 4, skip first st, skip CL, dc in top of ch-2 turning ch.

Repeat Rows 3 and 4 to desired length.

FRINGED BELT

With smaller hook, make Basic Blobble Belt. Pictured belt is 48"/122cm before fringe added.

Add Fringe

Cut 12 strands of yarn 33"/84cm long. Holding 6 strands together, thread through center stitch at one end of belt. Bring opposite ends of all strands together to ensure equal length. Holding all ends together (including beginning tail), tie an overhand knot. Trim fringe to approximately 8"/20.5cm long, and tightly knot end of each strand. Repeat for other end of belt.

SEQUINED BELT

With larger hook, and 1 strand each of Jelly yarn and sequined thread held together, make Basic Blobble Belt, leaving only 4"/10cm beginning yarn tail. Pictured belt is 60"/152.5cm long.

This belt needs to be handled more gently so that the sequins do not snag on each other. If sequins snag, stretch nearest jelly yarn stitches to ease sequin thread back into place. Keep in mind that sequin thread is not elastic. A longer belt is recommended for this style to allow for tying rather than feeding one belt end through chain spaces of other end, which tends to snag the sequins.

BLING BELT

With smaller hook, make Basic Blobble Belt. Pictured belt is 43"/109cm long before gems added.

Embellish End

Fasten off leaving an 18"/45.5cm yarn tail. With tail, ch 2 tightly, string a jumbo drop-style bead and bring up close to hook, ch 1, hdc in top of last turning ch. String smaller bead on end of tail and push into chain space just created. Knot and weave tail into end of belt. Secure bead with spot of glue.

Embellish Beginning

String one smaller bead, one jumbo bead, and one more smaller bead onto tail and weave tail back into first row so that the beads hang evenly from belt end. Knot and secure tail with glue. When glue is dry, trim tails.

This project was created with

1 ball each of Yummy Yarns' Jelly Yarn, 100% vinyl, 8½oz/240g = 65yd/60m, in Hot Pink Candy, Blue Taffy, and Lemon-Lime Ice

Embellishments

Sequined Belt: Berroco Lazer FX, 100% polyester, 10g = 70yd/64m in color #6005 Jeweltones.

Bling Belt: ACI Sparkling Gems (UPC 7-26906-12651-3) and Darice Inc. Acrylic Bead Crystal-Asst. (UPC 0-82676-37499-9)

Madcap
Accessories

Bland-busting accessories
for the unconventional

Funky Felted Laptop Bag & PSP Cozy

Most laptop bags are so very utilitarian. Chuck the norm and stash your favorite high-tech toys in stylish bags as individual as yourself. Bold stripes of felting wool and eyelash yarn are felted to form these dense, sturdy, fashion-forward cases.

Designer: **Kalpna Kapoor**

SKILL LEVEL
Intermediate

FINISHED MEASUREMENTS
15½" x 14"/39.5 x 35.5 cm before felting

14" x 13½"/35.5 x 34.5 cm after felting

YOU WILL NEED (FOR ONE LAPTOP BAG AND ONE PSP COZY)
Approx 400yd/366m worsted weight 100% felting wool, black (A)

Approx 400yd/366m worsted weight 100% felting wool, pink (B)

Approx 400yd/366m worsted weight 100% felting wool, green (C)

Approx 200yd/183m eyelash yarn, orange (D)

Hook: 5.5mm/I-9 or size needed to obtain gauge

Stitch markers

FELTING SUPPLIES
Washing machine (preferably top loading)

Lingerie bag or pillow protector

Jeans or towels (for added agitation)

Mild detergent

STITCHES USED
Chain (ch)

Half double crochet (hdc)

Slip stitch (sl st)

GAUGE
Take time to check your gauge.

12 hdc and 10 rows = 4"/10cm with two strands of A held together.

PATTERN NOTES
Be sure to use 100% wool that is appropriate for felting; do not use super wash.

To change color, work last stitch to where there are 2 loops on hook, yarn over with new color to complete stitch.

LAP TOP BAG

With two strands of A held together, ch 45.

Row 1: Hdc in 2nd ch from hook and in each ch across (44 hdc).

Row 2: Hdc in each st across.

Rnd 3: Hdc in each st across to end of row; rotate piece to work along short side, work 2 hdc evenly spaced along side; rotate piece to work in free loops of foundation chain, hdc in each free loop of foundation chain; rotate piece to work along other short side, work 2 hdc evenly spaced along side; do not join (92 hdc).

Work now progresses in continuous spirals. Mark beginning of next round and move marker as each new round is started.

Rnd 4: Hdc in each st around.

Rnd 5: Hdc in each st around; change to two strands of B in last st.

Rnds 6—8: Hdc in each st around; change to one strand each of C and D in last st.

Rnds 9—11: Hdc in each st around; change to two strands of A in last st.

Rnds 12—14: Hdc in each st around; change to one strand each of B and D in last st.

Rnds 15—17: Hdc in each st around; change to two strands of C in last st.

Rnds 18—26: Repeat Rnds 9—17.

Rnds 27—29: Hdc in each st around; change to two strands of A in last st.

Rnd 30: Hdc in each st around.

Rnd 31: Hdc in next 13 sts, ch 15, skip 15 sts (handle space made), hdc in next 31 sts, ch 15, skip 15 sts (handle space), hdc in each st around.

Rnd 32: Hdc in each st and ch around (92 hdc).

Rnd 33: Hdc in each st around; sl st in next st at end of round to join. Fasten off and weave in ends.

PSP COZY

With two strands of A held together, ch 18.

Rnd 1: Hdc in 2nd ch from hook and in each ch across; rotate piece to work along opposite side of foundation chain, hdc in each free loop of foundation chain; do not join (34 hdc).

Work progresses in continuous spirals. Mark beginning of next round and move marker as each new round is started.

Rnd 2: Hdc in each st around; change to two strands of B in last st.

Rnds 3 and 4: Hdc in each st around; change to one strand each of C and D in last st.

Rnds 5 and 6: Hdc in each st around; change to two strands of A in last st.

Rnds 7 and 8: Hdc in each st around; change to one strand each of B and D in last st.

Rnds 9 and 10: Hdc in each st around; change to two strands of C in last st.

Rnds 11—16: Repeat Rnds 5—10.

Rnd 17: Hdc in each st around.

Rnd 18: Hdc in next 6 sts, ch 7, skip 7 sts (handle space made), hdc in next 10 sts, ch 7, skip 7 sts (handle space), hdc in each st around.

Rnd 19: Hdc in each st and ch around; sl st in next st at end of round to join. Fasten off and weave in ends.

FELTING

Using washer (preferably top-loading, so you can check on the bags and stop and start the cycles), set washing temperature on hot (the hottest water yields the best results; turn up water heater, if necessary). Use the least amount of water possible (small load setting, for example). Add a tablespoon of detergent. Place each bag in a separate zippered pillow protector or lingerie bag and put them in the washer along with jeans or towels. The jeans and towels help with the agitation and speed up the felting time. Agitate for about 10 minutes (the actual time will vary with each washer).

Before felting

Depending on the length of your wash cycle, you may need to start the cycle over a few times. Don't drain or spin between agitation cycles. Remove from washer when all the stitches have disappeared and the wool feels firm. Rinse thoroughly with cold water. Wrap in a dry towel and squeeze to remove more moisture. Shape bag and cozy, stuff with plastic bags to hold shape, and allow to air dry.

This project was created with
2 balls of Plymouth's Galway, 100% pure wool, 3 1/2oz/100g = 210yd/192m, color #9.

2 balls of Plymouth's Galway, 100% pure wool, 3½oz/100g = 210yd/192m, color #141.

2 balls of Plymouth's Galway, 100% pure wool, 3 1/2oz/100g = 210yd/192m, color #130.

2 balls of Lana Grossa Basics' Venezia, 100% polyester, 1¾oz/50g = 98yd/90m, color #001.

Coffee Service for One

Designer: **Vashti Braha**

This clever little coffee sleeve is perfect for java drinkers on the go. Double-faced single crochet produces a double layer fabric, and when combined with color changes, yields a sleeve fully equipped with insulating layers, sweetener/creamer pockets, and stirrer loops. All this and very few yarn ends to weave in.

SKILL LEVEL
Intermediate/Advanced

FINISHED MEASUREMENTS
Bottom circumference: 3½"/9cm
Top circumference: 4½"/11.5cm

YOU WILL NEED
Approx 100yd/92m fingering weight
    wool, outside color (A)
Approx 100yd/92m fingering weight
    wool, inside color (B)
Hook: 3.5mm/E-4 or size needed to ob-
    tain gauge
Yarn needle

STITCHES USED
Chain (ch)
Half double crochet (hdc)
Single crochet (sc)
Slip stitch (sl st)
Double-faced single crochet (dfsc)
Single crochet decrease (sc2tog)

GAUGE
Take time to check your gauge.
20 dfsc and 20 rows = 4"/10cm

PATTERN NOTES

To change color, pull new color through loop of old color on hook, pull old color to tighten and drop strand without fastening off.

Right side rows are worked in A, and wrong side rows are worked in B. Row numbers are designated A or B to indicate the color and side (right or wrong) of pattern. For example, Row 3A is the 3rd row on the right side; Row 3B is the 3rd row on the wrong side.

Working double-faced stitches may require holding the fabric in a different position. For comfort, try holding the fabric sideways or even upside down.

When working double-faced stitches, passing the hook in front of the working yarn, before inserting the hook into the next stitch, produces a slightly different look than passing the hook behind the working yarn. Both methods produce a double-faced single crochet of appropriate gauge. For a consistent look, be sure to always pass the hook on the same side of the working yarn before inserting into the next st.

When working with double-faced stitches, an increase takes two rows to complete. In the first row, 2 stitches are worked in a single stitch. In the next row, 1 stitch is worked in each of the 2 stitches, but the hook is inserted in the free loop of the same stitch in the row below.

COFFEE SLEEVE
Do not crochet over yarn tails.

With B, leaving a 4"/10cm tail, ch 39 loosely.

Row 1 (RS is in color B this row only): Sc in one loop of 2nd ch from hook and in one loop of each ch across (38 sc).

Row 1B (WS): Ch 1, turn, insert hook in back loop of first sc and free loop of corresponding foundation chain, draw yarn through both loops, yarn over and draw through both loops on hook (dfsc made), * insert hook in back loop of next sc and free loop of corresponding foundation chain, draw yarn through both loops, yarn over and draw through both loops on hook; repeat from * across (38 dfsc).

Change to A. Do not fasten off B.

Row 2A: Ch 1, turn, dfsc in each st across (38 dfsc).

Fold strip in half with A facing out. Tie yarn tails together to join rows into a ring (to be seamed later).

Change to B. Do not fasten off A.

Row 2B: Ch 1, turn, dfsc in each st across.

Continue to change color at end of each row; use A on right side of coffee sleeve, B on wrong side. Gently pull edges of ring together when changing color.

Row 3A: Ch 1, turn, dfsc in first 8 sts, 2 dfsc in next st (increase begun), dfsc in next 20 sts, 2 dfsc in next st (increase begun), dfsc in last 8 sts (40 dfsc).

Row 3B: Ch 1, turn, dfsc in first 8 sts, dfsc in next 2 sts inserting hook in same st in row below (increase completed), dfsc in next 10 sts, ch 5, dfsc in next st (stirrer loop), dfsc in next 9 sts, dfsc in next 2 sts inserting hook in same st in row below (increase completed), dfsc in last 8 sts.

Row 4A: Ch 1, turn, dfsc in first 19 sts, ch 2, skip (dfsc, ch 5, dfsc) and 2 sts one row below, dfsc in last 19 sts (38 dfsc).

Row 4B: Ch 1, turn, dfsc in first 6 sts, 2 sc in front loop only of next 9 sts (first pocket begun), dfsc in next 4 sts; working in stirrer loop, sc in first dfsc, sl st in 5 ch, sc in next dfsc; skip 2 ch of Row 4A, dfsc in next 4 sts, 2 sc in front loop only of next 9 sts (second pocket begun), dfsc in last 6 sts.

Pull stirrer loop through from WS to RS under ch-2 space.

Row 5A: Ch 1, turn, dfsc in first 6 sts; inserting hook in free loop of next st and free loop of st in row below, work hdc in each of next 9 sts to form back of pocket; dfsc in next st, 2 dfsc in next st, dfsc in next 2 sts, 2 sc in ch-2 space behind stirrer loop, dfsc in next 2 sts, 2 dfsc in next st, dfsc in next st; inserting hook in free loop of next st and free loop of st in row below, work hdc in each of next 9 sts to form back of pocket; dfsc in last 6 sts (42 sts).

Row 5B: Ch 1, turn, dfsc in first 6 sts, sc in next 18 sc, dfsc in next 5 sts, sc in back loop only of next 2 sc, dfsc in next 5 sts, sc in next 18 sc, dfsc in last 6 sts.

Row 6A: Ch 1, turn, (dfsc in each st to pocket, sc in back loop only of 9 sts forming back of pocket) twice, dfsc in each remaining st.

Row 6B: Ch 1, turn, (dfsc in each st to pocket, sc in each sc across pocket) twice, dfsc in each st across.

Rows 7A and 7B: Repeat Rows 6A and 6B.

Row 8A: Repeat Row 6A, working 2 dfsc in the 5th and 38th sts (44 sts).

Row 8B: Ch 1, turn, dfsc in each st to pocket, sc in each sc across pocket, dfsc in next 6 sts, ch 5, dfsc in next st (stirrer loop), dfsc in each st to pocket, sc in each sc across pocket, dfsc in each remaining st.

Row 9A: Ch 1, turn, dfsc in each st to pocket, sc in back loop only of 9 sts forming back of pocket, dfsc in each st to stirrer loop, ch 2, skip stirrer loop, dfsc in each st to pocket, sc in back loop only of 9 sts forming back of pocket, dfsc in each remaining st.

Row 9B: Ch 1, turn, dfsc in each st to pocket, sc in each sc across pocket, dfsc in next 5 sts; working in stirrer loop, sc in first dfsc, sl st in 5 ch, sc in next dfsc; skip 2 ch of Row 9A, dfsc in next 5 sts, sc in each sc across pocket, dfsc in each remaining st.

Pull stirrer loop through from WS to RS under ch-2 space.

Row 10A: Ch 1, turn, dfsc in each st to pocket, sc in back loop only of 9 sts forming back of pocket, dfsc in next 5 sts, 2 sc in ch-2 space behind stirrer

loop, dfsc in each st to pocket, sc in back loop only of 9 sts forming back of pocket, dfsc in each remaining st (44 sts).

Row 10B: Ch 1, turn, dfsc in each st to pocket, sc in each sc across pocket, dfsc in next 5 sts, sc in back loop only of next 2 sc, dfsc in each st to pocket, sc in each sc across pocket, dfsc in each remaining st.

Rows 11A, 11B, 12A, 12B and 13A: Repeat Rows 6A and 6B twice, then repeat Row 6A (44 sts).

Row 13B: Ch 1, turn, dfsc in each st to pocket, sc2tog 3 times, sc in next 6 sc, sc2tog 3 times, dfsc in next 6 sts, ch 5, dfsc in next st (stirrer loop), dfsc in next 5 sts, sc2tog 3 times, sc in next 6 sc, sc2tog 3 times, dfsc in each remaining st.

Row 14A: Ch 1, turn, dfsc in each st to pocket, hdc in each of 9 sts forming back of pocket, dfsc in each st to stirrer loop, ch 2, skip stirrer loop, dfsc in each st to pocket, hdc in each of 9 sts forming back of pocket, dfsc in each remaining st.

Row 14B: Ch1, turn, dfsc in each st to pocket, sc in back loop only of each hdc forming back of pocket, dfsc in next 5 sts; working in stirrer loop, sc in first dfsc, sl st in 5 ch, sc in next dfsc; skip 2 ch, dfsc in next 5 sts, sc in back loop only of each hdc forming back of pocket, dfsc in each remaining st.

Pull stirrer loop through from WS to RS under ch-2 space.

Row 15A: Ch 1, turn, dfsc in each st to stirrer loop, 2 sc in ch-2 space behind stirrer loop, dfsc in each remaining st (44 sts).

Row 15B: Ch 1, turn, dfsc in each st to stirrer loop, sc in back loop only of next 2 sc, dfsc in each remaining st.

Row 16A: Ch 1, turn, dfsc in each st across.

For a taller coffee sleeve, repeat Row 16A (alternating colors as established) until sleeve is desired height.

Row 16B: Ch 1, turn, dfsc in each st across; join with sl st in first st.

Edging Row (optional)
Do not turn, with color B and RS facing, * insert hook in free loop of next st in Row 16A and free loop of next st in Row 16B, yarn over and draw through all 3 loops on hook (sl st completed), ch 1; working loosely, repeat from * around; join with sl st in first sl st.

Inside Seam
Sl st loosely along inside seam to RS bottom edge.

Repeat Edging Row (optional)
Along bottom edge inserting hook in free loop of foundation chain and horizontal strand of each sc of Row 1A. Fasten off.

Outside Seam
With A, sl st down front of seam or sew seam closed.

Weave in ends.

This project was created with
1 ball each of Louet Sales' Gems Pearl, 100% merino wool, super fine (fingering) weight 1¾oz/50g = 185yd/170m in colors 80-1472-7 Terra Cotta and 80-1622-3 Citrus, or 80-1562-9 Navy and 80-1022-7 Ginger

Bag of Armor

It's a tough world out there. Now there's a tough bag for toting all your survival gear. Better yet, this Bag of Armor can be crocheted quickly and easily with basic stitches and material found at your local hardware store.

Designer: **Tammy Hildebrand**

SKILL LEVEL
Easy

FINISHED MEASUREMENTS
Height: 15"/38cm
Circumference: 25"/64cm

YOU WILL NEED
Approx 50yd/46m 1¾"/44mm woven
   polypropylene duct support strap or
   webbing (not duct tape), gray/silver
Hook: 16mm/Q-19 or size needed to
   obtain gauge

STITCHES USED
Chain (ch)
Double crochet (dc)
Single crochet (sc)
Slip stitch (sl st)

GAUGE
Take time to check your gauge.
11 dc = 3½"/9cm and 10 rows dc =
   4"/10cm

PATTERN NOTES
Strapping must first be cut into narrower
strips, as follows:

Cut strapping in half lengthwise. Cut each
strip in half again to create 4 strips. Wind
each strip into a ball and secure with a
rubber band.

When cutting strapping, work with man-
ageable lengths. Wind strips into balls as
you go.

BAG
Ch 4; join with sl st in first ch to form
ring.

Rnd 1: Ch 3 (counts as dc here and
   throughout), work 11 dc in ring; join
   with sl st in top of beginning ch 3 (12
   dc).

Rnd 2: Ch 3, dc in same st as join, 2 dc
   in each st around; join with sl st in top
   of beginning ch 3 (24 dc).

Rnd 3: Ch 1, sc in each st around; join
   with sl st in beginning sc.

Rnds 4—11: Ch 3, dc in each st
   around; join with sl st in top of beginning ch 3. Do not fasten off; proceed
   with Handle.

Handle
Row 1: Ch 1, sc in first 3 sts; leave
   remaining sts unworked (3 sc).

Rows 2—26: Ch 1, turn, sc in
   each of 3 sts across.

Centering handle across
top of bag and leaving 9
unworked sts on each
side, sl st last row
of handle to last
round of bag.

Fasten off.

This project was created with
½ roll of 100% polypropylene monofila-
ment support webbing, 1¾"/44mm x
100yd/91m, color Silver.

Two-Liter Purse

Make a couple of great little purses with a small amount of ribbon yarn, recycled plastic soda pop bottles, and the simplest of crochet stitches. The smaller coin purse nestles conveniently inside the larger purse, and the clear plastic lets you see instantly whether you have enough change for the parking meter.

Designer: **Jen Neitzel**

SKILL LEVEL
Easy

FINISHED MEASUREMENTS
Large Purse: 6" x 3½"/15 x 9cm
(without handle)
Small Purse: 3¼" x 2¼"/8 x 6cm

YOU WILL NEED (FOR LARGE PURSE)
Approx 95yd/87m light worsted weight
ribbon yarn, color of your choice

YOU WILL NEED (FOR SMALL PURSE)
Approx 45yd/41m light worsted weight
ribbon yarn, color of your choice
Hook: 5mm/H-8 or size needed to
obtain gauge

One 2-liter plastic soft drink bottle
(for large purse)
One 20oz plastic soft drink bottle
(for small purse)
Scissors
Craft knife
Permanent marker
Tape measure or ruler
Hole punch

STITCHES USED
Chain (ch)
Single crochet (sc)
Slip stitch (sl st)

GAUGE
Take time to check your gauge.
First 6 rnds = 3¼"/8.5cm in diameter.

PREPARE SOFT DRINK BOTTLES

Before starting, wash soft drink bottles
and remove labels. Remove any inked
markings with soap or non-abrasive
cleaner. With scissors or craft knife
remove top, rounded part, and bottom
of bottle, then cut along outside of glue
seams on bottle, removing the seam
completely (figure 1). This will yield a
long, curled rectangle. Use scissors to
round all four corners.

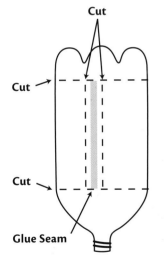

Figure 1

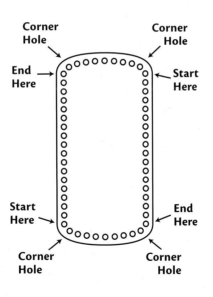

Figure 2

LARGE PURSE
With permanent marker, mark 18 dots
evenly spaced along each long edge of
bottle. Mark dots about 5/16"/.8mm from
edge. Mark dots evenly spaced along
short edges of bottle (figure 2). Use hole
punch to make a hole at each dot.

Purse End (make 2)
Ch 4; join with sl st in first ch to form ring.

Work progresses in continuous spirals;
do not join rounds (unless otherwise
instructed). Mark beginning of first round,
and move marker as each new round
is started.

Rnd 1: Work 9 sc in ring (9 sc).

Rnd 2: 2 sc in each st around (18 sc).

Rnd 3: Sc in each st around.

Handle

Ch 40, taking care to not twist chain; join with sc in st on opposite side of purse opening.

Row 1: Ch 1, turn, sc in each ch across; join with sl st in next st on opposite edge of purse.

Fasten off. Weave in end and use to reinforce corner sts.

SMALL PURSE

With permanent marker, mark 13 dots evenly spaced along each long edge of bottle. Mark dots about $5/16$"/.8mm from edge. Mark dots evenly spaced along short edges of bottle. Use hole punch to make a hole at each dot.

Purse End (make 2)

Ch 4; join with sl st in first ch to form ring.

Work progresses in continuous spirals; do not join rounds (unless otherwise instructed). Mark beginning of first round and move marker as each new round is started.

Rnds 1—4: Work Rnds 1-4 of Large Purse End (36 sc).

Rnd 5: Sc in first 6 sts, * 2 sc in next st, sc in next 11 sts; repeat from * one more time, 2 sc in next st, sc in last 5 sts (39 sc).

ASSEMBLY

Single crochet is used to attach the Purse Ends to the edges of the plastic rectangle. Gently curve the plastic rectangle into a cylinder as work progresses. 3 single crochet (and 3 sts of the Purse

Rnd 4: 2 sc in each st around (36 sc).

Rnds 5 and 6: Sc in each st around. Do not fasten off.

ASSEMBLY

Single crochet is used to attach the Purse Ends to the edges of the plastic rectangle. Gently curve the plastic rectangle into a cylinder as work progresses. 2 single crochet (and 2 sts of the Purse End) are worked in each hole around the edge of the plastic.

Rnd 1: Insert hook in next st of Purse End and in first hole on long side of plastic rectangle, yarn over and draw up loop, yarn over and draw through both loops on hook (single crochet made), work another sc in next st of Purse End and same hole of plastic

rectangle, * work sc in next st of Purse End and next hole of plastic rectangle, work sc in next st of Purse End and same hole of plastic rectangle; repeat from * around; 4 sc in corner hole of plastic rectangle, 2 sc in each hole of short side of plastic rectangle across to other corner hole, 4 sc in corner hole, sc in first hole on other long side of plastic rectangle. Fasten off. Weave in end and use to reinforce corner sts.

Repeat to attach second Purse End to other long end of plastic rectangle. Join with sl st in first st of Rnd 1. Do not fasten off.

End) are worked in each hole around the edge of the plastic.

Rnd 1: Insert hook in next st of Purse End and in first hole on long side of plastic rectangle, yarn over and draw up loop, yarn over and draw through both loops on hook (single crochet made), (work sc in next st of Purse End and same hole of plastic rectangle) twice, * work sc in next st of Purse End and next hole of plastic rectangle, (work sc in next st and same hole) twice; repeat from * around; 4 sc in corner hole of plastic rectangle, 3 sc in each hole of short side of plastic rectangle across to other corner hole, 4 sc in corner hole,

sc in first hole on other long side of plastic rectangle. Fasten off. Weave in end and use to reinforce corner sts.

Repeat to attach second Purse End to other long end of plastic rectangle. Join with sl st in first st of Rnd 1. Fasten off. Weave in end and use to reinforce corner sts.

This project was created with
1 skein of Needful's Elba, 100% nylon, 1¾oz/50g = 153yd/140m, color #2157

Emoticon Bag

Here's a bag that will express your emotional states: all of them. Single crochet squares are embroidered and embellished with chains to create 12 different emoticons. And making it will undoubtedly put you in a good mood :)

Designer: **Nanette M. Seale**

SKILL LEVEL
Easy

FINISHED MEASUREMENTS
16" x 13" x 2½"/41 x 33 x 6.5cm bag
33½" x 2½"/85 x 6cm strap

YOU WILL NEED
Approx 165yd/151m worsted weight
    cotton yarn, black (A)
Approx 380yd/348m worsted weight
    cotton yarn, gray (B)
Approx 145yd/133m worsted weight
    cotton yarn, white (C)
Hook: 4.5mm/G-7 or size needed to
    obtain gauge
Yarn needle

STITCHES USED
Chain (ch)
Single crochet (sc)
Slip stitch (sl st)

SPECIAL TECHNIQUE
Double ring method (page 000)
GAUGE
Take time to check your gauge.
1 motif = 3½"/9cm square
15 sc and 16 rows sc = 4"/10cm

SQUARE (MAKE 8 IN EACH OF A, B, AND C)
Ch 13.

Row 1: Sc in 2nd ch from hook and each ch across (12 sc).

Rows 2—12: Ch 1, turn, sc in each sc across.

Rnd 13: Ch 1, turn, sc evenly around square working 1 sc in each st and end of each row, and 3 sc in each corner; join with sl st in first sc. Fasten off.

EMOTICON FACES

PATTERN NOTE
When working on A square, make face with C. When working on B or C square, make face with A.

Smiley Face (make 2 with A on C squares)
Small Eye (make 2): Form a ring using the double ring method. Work 3 sc in ring; tighten ring and join with sl st in first st. Fasten off. Sew eyes to square about 3 sts apart.

Standard Nose: Embroider two chain stitches over the center sts of Rows 5 and 6.

Smiley Mouth: Ch 10. Fasten off. Sew mouth to square in a smile shape.

Large-Eye Smiley Face (make 2 with A on B squares)
Large Eye (make 2): Form a ring using the double ring method. Work 6 sc in ring; tighten ring and join with sl st in first st. Fasten off. Sew eyes to square about 3 sts apart.

Mouth: Make Smiley Mouth.

Straight-Brow Smiley Face (make 2 with A on C squares)
Eye: Ch 5. Fasten off. Sew in a straight line between second and third rows of square.

Standard Nose: Embroider Standard Nose.

Mouth: Make Smiley Mouth.

Winking Smiley Face (make 2 with C on A squares)
Winking Eye (make 1): Ch 3. Fasten off. Sew in a straight line between second and third rows.

Nose: Embroider Standard Nose.

Mouth: Make Smiley Mouth.

Small-Eye Grimacing Face (make 2 with C on A squares)
Eyes: Make 2 Small Eyes.

Nose: Embroider Standard Nose.

Mouth: Ch 12. Fasten off. Sew mouth to square in a squiggly grimace shape.

Angry Face (make 2 with A on B squares)

Eyebrow and Mouth (make 2): Ch 7. Fasten off. Sew Eyebrow in a V shape in center of Rows 1—3 of square. Sew Mouth in an upside-down V in center of Rows 9—11.

Eyes: Make 2 Small Eyes.

Nose: Embroider Standard Nose over the center sts of Rows 6 and 7.

Surprise Face (make 2 with A on C squares)

Eyes: Make 2 Small Eyes.

Nose: Embroider Standard Nose.

Mouth: Ch 12; join with sl st in first ch to form ring. Fasten off. Sew to square in an oval shape.

Frowny Face (make 2 with A on C squares)

Eyes: Make 2 Small Eyes.

Mouth: Ch 12. Fasten off. Sew to square in a frown over Rows 8—10.

Talking Face (make 2 with C on A squares)

Eyes: Make 2 Small Eyes.

Mouth (make 2): Ch 7. Fasten off. Sew pieces to square over Rows 7—8 and 9—11; one in a smile shape, the other in an upside down smile shape. They should be one on top of the other with one row between them at the edges of the mouth.

Sour Face (make 2 with A on B squares)

Eyes: Make 2 Small Eyes.

Nose: Embroider Standard Nose.

Mouth (make 2): Ch 5. Fasten off. Sew to square in an X shape over center of Rows 9—11.

Blinking Face (make 2 with A on B squares)

Eyes (make 2): Ch 3. Fasten off. Sew to square over Rows 3—5 slanting inwards and with 2 sts between eyes at bottom.

Mouth: Ch 3. Fasten off. Sew to square over center between Rows 8—9.

Sleeping Face (make 2 with C on A)

Eyes (make 2): Ch 5. Fasten off. Sew to square over Rows 2—3 in a curved shape.

Mouth: Make Smiley Mouth.

SIDES

With B, ch 8.

Row 1: Sc in 2nd ch from hook and each ch across (7 sc).

Rows 2—150: Ch 1, turn, sc in each st across.

Rnd 151: Ch 1, turn, sc evenly around square working 1 sc in each st and end of each row, and 3 sc in each corner; join with sl st in first sc. Fasten off.

ASSEMBLY

Sew squares together to make Front and Back of bag. Refer to diagrams for color arrangement.

Front **Back**

Sewing through back loops, sew edges of side piece to edges of sides and bottom of Front and Back pieces.

TOP EDGE

Join B with sc in any st at top of bag, sc evenly around top; join with sl st in first sc. Fasten off.

SHOULDER STRAP

With right side facing; join B with sc in first st at top of side piece.

Row 1: Sc in each st across.

Rows 2—115: Ch 1, turn, sc in each st across (7 sc). Fasten off. Sew Row 115 to top of other side of bag.

Strap Edging

With right side facing; join B with sc in side of first row of strap.

Rnd 1: Working in ends of rows, sc in each row across; working across top of bag, sc in each st across; join with sl st in first sc.

Rnd 2: Do not turn, sl st in each sc around; join with sl st in first sl st. Fasten off.

With right side facing; join B with sc in side of last row of strap. Repeat Rnds 1 and 2 on other side of strap.

This project was created with 3 skeins each of Elmore-Pisgah's Peaches & Crème, 100% cotton worsted weight yarn, 2½oz/70g = 120yd/110m, color #1 White, #2 Black, and #69 Silver Gray.

Skull and Crossbones Appliqués

Argh! Crochet is for everybody, matey! Sew these skull and crossbones onto a hat, jacket, backpack, or any wearable, and let everyone know that you're not an ordinary crochet fan. Who says thread crochet is only for doilies? Put metallic crochet thread to nontraditional use and create some of these versatile Jolly Roger appliqués.

Designer: **Joy Prescott**

96

SKULL

PATTERN NOTE

Reserve three small lengths, about 3yd/3m, of thread before starting. These lengths will be used when shaping mouth and eyes.

Ch 7.

Row 1: Sc in 2nd ch from the hook and each ch across (6 sc).

Row 2: Ch 1, turn, 2 sc in first st, sc in each st to last st, 2 sc in last st (8 sc).

Row 3: Ch 1, turn, 2 sc in first st, sc in each st to last st, 2 sc in last st (10 sc).

Row 4: Ch 1, turn, 3 sc in first st, sc in each st to last st, 3 sc in last st (14 sc).

Mouth
Shape Right Side of Mouth

Row 5: Ch 1, turn, sc in first 4 sts; leave remaining sts unworked (4 sc).

Rows 6—10: Ch 1, turn, sc in each st across (4 sc). Drop loop from hook, but do not fasten off.

Shape Left Side of Mouth
Skip 6 unworked sts on Row 4; join another small length of thread with sl st in next st.

Row 5: Ch 1, sc in same st and in next 3 sts (4 sc).

Rows 6—10: Ch 1, turn, sc in each st across (4 sc). Fasten off.

Complete Mouth
Pick up dropped loop on right side of mouth.

Row 11: Ch 1, turn, sc in each st across Right Side of Mouth, ch 12, sc in each st on Left Side of Mouth.

Row 12: Ch 1, turn, 2 sc in first st, sc in next 3 sts, sc in next 5 ch, sc2tog over next 2 ch, sc in next 5 ch, sc in next 3 sts, 2 sc in last st (21 sts).

Rows 13—15: Ch 1, turn, sc in each st across.

Row 16: Ch 1, turn, sc in first 8 sts, ch 7 (nose opening), skip 5 sc, sc in next 8 sc.

Row 17: Ch 1, turn, 3 sc in first st, sc in next 7 sts, sc in next 3 ch, 3 sc in next ch, sc in next 3 ch, sc in next 7 sc, 3 sc in last st (29 sc).

Row 18: Ch 1, turn, sc in each st across.

Shape Right Eye Socket
Row 19: Ch 1, turn, 2 sc in first st, sc in next st, sc2tog; leave remaining sts unworked (4 sc).

Rows 20 and 21: Ch 1, turn, sc in each st across (4 sc).

Row 22: Ch 1, turn, 2 sc in first st, sc in next 2 sc, 2 sc in last st (6 sc).

Row 23: Ch 1, turn, sc in each st across.

Row 24: Ch 1, turn, 2 sc in first st, sc in each st across (7 sc). Drop loop from hook, but do not fasten off.

Shape Bridge of Nose

Skip 7 unworked sts on Row 18; join another small length of thread with sl st in next st.

Row 19: Ch 1, sc in same st and in next 6 sts; leave remaining sts unworked (7 sc).

Row 20: Ch 1, turn, sc in each sc across (7 sc).

Row 21: Ch 1, turn, 2 sc in first st, sc in each st across to last st, 2 sc in last st (9 sc).

Row 22: Ch 1, turn, sc in each st across.

Rows 23 and 24: Repeat Rows 21-22 (11 sc). Fasten off.

Shape Left Eye Socket

Skip 7 unworked sts on Row 18; join another small length of thread with sl st in next st.

Row 19: Ch 1, work sc2tog over same and next st, sc in next st, 2 sc in last st (4 sc).

Rows 20 and 21: Ch 1, turn, sc in each st across.

Row 22: Ch 1, turn, 2 sc in first st, sc in next 2 sts, 2 sc in last st (6 sc).

Row 23: Ch 1, turn, sc in each st across.

Row 24: Ch 1, turn, sc in each st across to last st, 2 sc in last st (7 sc). Fasten off.

Complete Eyes

Pick up dropped loop from Right Eye Socket shaping.

Row 25: Ch 1, turn, sc in each st of right side of eye socket, ch 3, sc in each st of nose bridge, ch 3, sc in each st of left side of eye socket.

Row 26: Ch 1, turn, sc in each st and ch across (31 sc).

Rows 27 and 28: Ch 1, turn, sc in each st across.

Row 29: Ch 1, turn, sc2tog over first 2 sts, sc in each st across to last 2 sts, sc2tog (29 sc).

Row 30: Ch 1, turn, sc in each st across.

Rows 31 and 32: Repeat Rows 29 and 30 (27 sc).

Rows 33—41: Repeat Row 29 (9 sc).

Rnd 42: Ch 1, do not turn, working around skull, sc in each row and st around; join with sl st in first sc. Fasten off.

Mouth and Eye Socket Edging

Join thread with sl st in any st around opening.

Rnd 1: Ch 1, sc in each row and st around; join with sl st in first sc. Fasten off.

Weave in ends.

CROSSBONE (MAKE 2)

Ch 5.

Row 1: Sc in 2nd ch from hook and in each ch across (4 sc).

Rows 2—41: Ch 1, turn, sc in each st across.

Row 42: Ch 1, turn, 2 sc in first st, sc in each st across to last st, 2 sc in last st (6 sc).

Row 43: Ch 1, turn, sc in each st across to last st, 2 sc in last st (7 sc).

Rows 44 and 45: Ch 1, turn, sc in each st across.

Row 46: Ch 1, turn, sc in first 4 sts, sl st in next st, sc in next 2 sts.

Row 47: Ch 1, turn, sc in first 2 sts, sl st in next st, sc in last 4 sts. Fasten off.

Other End of Crossbone

With wrong side of Row 1 facing, join thread with sl st in first st on opposite side of foundation chain.

Row 42: Ch 1, 2 sc in same st as join, sc in each st across to last st, 2 sc in last st (6 sc).

Rows 43—45: Ch 1, turn, sc in each st across.

Row 46: Ch 1, turn, sc in first 4 sts, sl st in next st, sc in next 2 sts.

Row 47: Ch 1, turn, sc in first 2 sts, sl st in next st, sc in last 4 sts.

Do not fasten off.

Rnd 48: Ch 1, do not turn, * working in ends of rows, sc in each row to opposite end of bone; working across last row of bone, 3 sc in first st, sc in each sc to sl st, sl st in sl st, sc in each sc to last st, 3 sc in last st; repeat from * once; join with sl st in first sc. Fasten off.

ASSEMBLY

Cross bones to create an X-shape. Use embroidery needle and crochet thread to tack bones together in center where they cross.

Crossbones may now be sewn behind or below skull. Alternately, bones and skull can be arranged and sewn on a hat, jacket, or bag.

This project was created with
1 ball of J&P Coats Royale size 10 metallic crochet thread, 93% cotton, 7% metallic, 100yd/92m, color #1s White/Silver

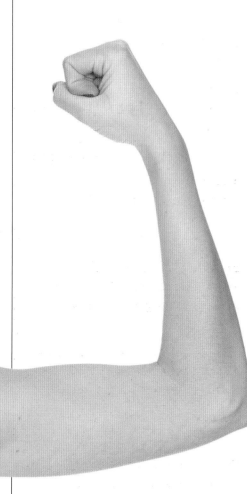

Summer Hat and Tote Combo

Whether clamming, collecting seashells, or strolling down the boardwalk, this hat and tote combo will come in handy, and will have your environmentally conscious friends applauding your ingenuity as well as your fashion sense. These clever, lightweight accessories are crocheted out of strips cut from plastic grocery bags. A big hook and basic crochet stitches make this a quick and easy project.

Designer: **Phyllis Sandford**

SKILL LEVEL
Easy

FINISHED MEASUREMENTS
Hat: One size fits most adults
Tote: 9"/23cm

FOR ONE HAT AND ONE TOTE YOU WILL NEED
Approx 20 plastic grocery bags, color of your choice (A)
Approx 10 plastic grocery bags, contrasting color of your choice (B)
Hook: 10mm/P-15 or size needed to obtain gauge
Stitch marker
6 medium seashells, about 1 3/4"/4.5cm long

7 small seashells, about 1"/2.5cm long
Sewing needle and matching thread
Cardboard in color to match main plastic bag color

STITCHES USED
Chain (ch)
Double crochet (dc)
Single crochet (sc)
Slip stitch (sl st)

GAUGE
Take time to check your gauge.
6 sc and 8 rows sc = 4"/10cm

PATTERN NOTES

To cut each bag into one long strip for crocheting, cut open one side seam, and then the bottom seam. Following the diagram below, cut on the dotted lines, starting and stopping where indicated. The corners can be trimmed after work is complete, if desired.

Work progresses in continuous spirals; do not join rounds (unless otherwise instructed). Mark beginning of first round and move marker as each new round is started.

To change color, work last stitch to where there are 2 loops on hook, yarn over with new color to complete stitch.

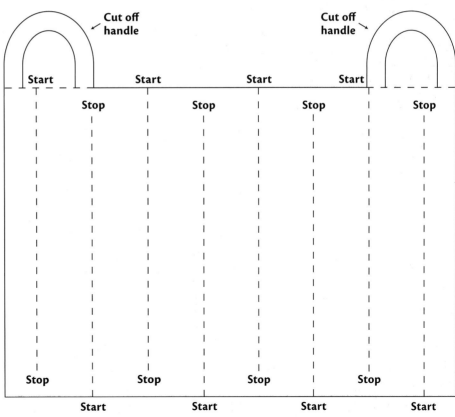

Cut off handle

Start

Stop

Start

Stop

Start

Stop

Start

Stop

Stop

Start

Stop

Start

Stop

Start

Stop

Start

Cut on dotted lines

TOTE

With A, ch 4; join with sl st in first ch to form a ring.

Rnd 1: Work 6 sc in ring; do not join; work in continuous spiral (6 sc).

Rnd 2: 2 sc in each st around (12 sc).

Rnd 3: * Sc in next st, 2 sc in next st; repeat from * 5 more times (18 sc).

Rnd 4: * Sc in next 2 sts, 2 sc in next st; repeat from * 5 more times (24 sc).

Rnd 5: * Sc in next 3 sts, 2 sc in next st; repeat from * 5 more times (30 sc).

Rnd 6: * Sc in next 4 sts, 2 sc in next st; repeat from * 5 more times; change to B in last st (36 sc).

Rnd 7: Sc in each st around.

Rnd 8: Ch 3 (counts as dc here and throughout), dc in each st around; join with sl st in top of beginning ch 3.

Rnd 9: Ch 3, dc in each st around; join with sl st in top of beginning ch 3; change to A in last st.

Rnds 10—12: Sc in each st around.

Rnd 13: Ch 5 (counts as dc, ch 2), * skip 2 sts, dc in next st, ch 2; repeat from * around; join with sl st in 3rd ch of beginning ch 5.

Rnd 14: Ch 3, 2 dc in ch-2 space of beginning ch-5, * dc in next st, 2 dc in next ch-2 space; repeat from * around; join with sl st in top of beginning ch 3.

Rnd 15: Sc in each st around.

Rnd 16: Sc in each st around; change to B in last st.

Rnd 17: Sc in each st around.

Rnd 18: Ch 5 (counts as dc, ch 2), *skip 2 sts, dc in next st, ch 2; repeat from * around.

Rnd 19: Sc in 3rd ch of ch-5, 2 sc in ch-2 space of beginning ch-5, *sc in next dc, 2 sc in next ch-2 space; repeat from * around.

Rnd 20—23: Sc in each st around. Fasten off.

Weave in all ends.

Bottom of Tote

From cardboard, cut a circle the same size as the bottom of the purse. Insert cardboard into purse.

Drawstring

With A, ch 62.

Row 1: Sc in 2nd ch from hook and each ch across (61 sc). Fasten off.

Weave in ends. Weave drawstring through ch-2 spaces of Rnd 18, pull to tighten, tie a knot at each end of the drawstring. To close Tote, tie ends of drawstring in a knot or bow.

Handle (make 2)

Join A with sc around any stitch in Rnd 16.

Row 1: Ch 24, sc around st in Rnd 16 about 5"/13cm from joining sc; turn, sc in each ch across, sl st around same st as join. Fasten off.

Repeat on opposite side of bag for 2nd handle.

Weave in all ends. Sew medium seashells evenly spaced around Rnd 20.

HAT

With A, ch 4; join with sl st in first ch to form a ring.

Rnds 1—5: Work Rnds 1—5 of Tote; change to B in last st.

Rnd 6: * Sc in next 4 sts, 2 sc in next st; repeat from * 5 more times (36 sc).

Rnds 7—11: Sc in each st around; change to A in last st.

Rnds 12—14: Sc in each st around.

Rnd 15: 2 sc in each st around (72 sc).

Rnds 16 and 17: Sc in each st around; change to B in last st of last rnd.

Rnd 18: 2 sc in each st around (144 sc).

Rnd 19: Sc in each st around; change to A in last st.

Rnd 20: Sc in each st around. Fasten off.

Weave in all ends. Sew small sea shells evenly spaced around Rnd 14.

This project was created with

20 recycled plastic grocery bags, white

10 recycled plastic grocery bags, yellow

Convertible Hat/Purse

A hat that carries your goodies, or a purse that you wear on your head? There's no need to choose: this pattern yields both in one. Triangles of single crochet are joined to form a dome. A drawstring woven through the edge allows the dome to be snugged to a custom-fitting cap, or closed completely to form a handy purse.

Designer: **Sharon Mann**

SKILL LEVEL
Beginner

FINISHED MEASUREMENTS
22"/56cm circumference
10"/25.5cm deep
15"/38cm wide

YOU WILL NEED
Approx 100yd/92m super bulky weight yarn, cap color (A)

Approx 100yd/92m super bulky weight yarn, contrasting cap color (B)

Approx 100yd/92m super bulky weight yarn, brim or edge color (C)

Hook: 8mm/L-11 or size needed to obtain gauge

Sewing needle and thread to match yarn colors

STITCHES USED
Chain (ch)
Double crochet (dc)
Single crochet (sc)
Slip stitch (sl st)

GAUGE
Take time to check your gauge.
8 sc and 8 rows sc = 4"/10cm

TRIANGLE (MAKE 4, 2 EACH IN A AND B)

Ch 2.

Row 1: 3 sc in 2nd ch from hook (3 sc).

Row 2: Ch 1, turn, 2 sc in first st, sc in next st, 2 sc in last st (5 sc).

Row 3: Ch 1, turn, sc in each st across.

Row 4: Ch 1, turn, 2 sc in first st, sc in next 3 sts, 2 sc in last st (7 sc).

Row 5: Ch 1, turn, sc in each st across.

Row 6: Ch 1, turn, 2 sc in first st, sc in next 5 sts, 2 sc in last st (9 sc).

Row 7: Ch 1, turn, sc in each st across.

Row 8: Ch 1, turn, 2 sc in first st, sc in next 7 sts, 2 sc in last st (11 sc).

Row 9: Ch 1, turn, sc in each st across. Fasten off and weave in ends.

ASSEMBLY

Using sewing needle and thread, sew triangles together with four points meeting at the top, to form a dome. Sew each seam twice for a secure hold.

Join C at edge of dome at the beginning of any triangle.

Rnd 1: Ch 3 (counts as dc here and throughout), work 43 dc evenly spaced around edge of dome; join with sl st in top of beginning ch 3 (44 dc).

Rnd 2: Ch 3, dc in each st around; join with sl st in top of beginning ch 3. Fasten off. Weave in ends.

Join B in top of ch 3 at beginning of Rnd 2.

Rnds 3 and 4: Ch 3, dc in each st around; join with sl st in top of begin-

ning ch 3. Fasten off. Weave in ends.

Join A in top of ch 3 at beginning of Rnd 4.

Rnd 5: Ch 1, sc in same st as join and each sc around; join with sl st in first st (44 sc).

Rnd 6: Ch 1, * sc in next st, 2 sc in next st; repeat from * around; join with sl st in first st (66 sc).

Rnd 7: Ch 3, skip first 3 sts, * sl st in next st, skip 1 st, ch 3; repeat from * around, skip last 2 sts; join with sl st in bottom of beginning ch 3 (32 ch-3 loops). Fasten off. Weave in ends.

Drawstring (make 2)
With B, ch 70. Fasten off.

Weave one drawstring in and out of ch-3 spaces on one side of Hat/Purse. Weave other drawstring in and out of ch-3 spaces on other side of Hat/Purse.

For Hat: Pull drawstrings slightly and tie a bow on either side of Hat.

For Purse: Pull drawstrings to cinch Purse closed, and tie ends of drawstrings together with overhand knots.

This project was created with
1 skein each of YLI's Shoelace Yarn, 100% acrylic, 6oz/168g = 100yd/92m, colors #W03 White and Royal, #W02 White and Orange, and #003 Royal

Gallery

NATHAN VINCENT

Fish, 2005.

10 x 20 x 4 inches
25 x 51 x 10 cm.

Chenille yam, spangles, polyfill, wire, wooden
mount, size H hook; double crochet.

Photo © Nathan Vincent

NATHAN VINCENT

Boxing Gloves, 2005.

12 x 12 x 4 inches
31 x 31 x 10 cm.

Worsted weight, acrylic yam, polyfill, wire
mesh, metal hook; half double crochet,
chain stitch, double crochet.

Photo © Nathan Vincent

NATHAN VINCENT

Beer, 2005.

12 x 9 x 12 inches
30 x 22.5 x 30 cm.

Worsted weight acrylic yarn, polyfill,
size H hook; half double crochet,
chain stitch embroidery.

Photo © Nathan Vincent

JENNY DOWDE

"Fancy That" Tea Cosy, 2005

18 x 8 inches
45 x 20 cm.

Wool blend, various fancy yarns, 4mm hook,
5mm hook; chain stitch, double crochet, treble
crochet, half treble crochet.

Photo © Tim Connelly
Images taken from 'Free Formations,' Published in 2006
by Sally Milner Publishing.

PATRICIA WALLER

Gnome, 2002

24 inches (height)
61 cm.

Yarn, polystyrene, synthetic material; crochet.

Photo © Patricia Waller

PATRICIA WALLER

Dentures, 1997.

8 inches (height)
20 cm.

Yarn, cotton wool, glass, glycerin; crochet.

Photo © Patricia Waller

ELAINE BRADFORD

By the Fire, 2004

77 x 44 x 21 inches
196 x 112 x 53 cm.

Mounted deer head, worsted weight
acrylic yarn, buttons, faux fireplace,
6mm hook; double crochet, sewn at seams.

Photo © Elaine Bradford

ELAINE BRADFORD

Rear Bumper Sweater, 2005

6 x 75 x 6 inches
15 x 190 x 15 cm.

Worsted weight acrylic yarn, buttons, hook-and-loop
fastener, 6.5mm hook; double crochet, single crochet.

Photo © Elaine Bradford
Courtesy Seth's Bumper Gallery, Houston, Texas.

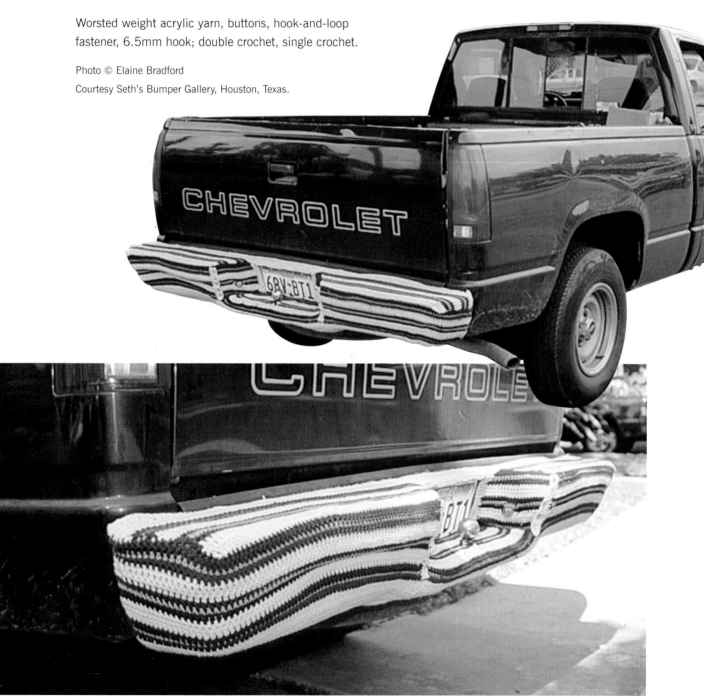

Designer Bios

Vashti Braha currently serves on the board of directors for the Crochet Guild of America (CGOA). Her designs, whether kooky or serious fashion, can be found in various crochet books, magazines, and CGOA's own Pattern Line at www.crochet.org. When she's not busy exploring crochet's limitless potentials, she maintains the blog http://designingvashti.blogspot.com, meets as many crocheters as possible at CGOA conferences and online, and helps her young son design his own quirky toys.

Drew Emborsky studied fine art at Kendall College of Art & Design in Grand Rapids, Michigan. He is an Associate Professional member of the Crochet Guild of America where he earned a master in basic stitches certificate. His patterns can be found at www.lulu.com/thecrochetdude as well as in national magazines. His wildly popular blog can be found at www.thecrochetdude.blogspot.com. Drew resides in Houston, Texas with his two cats Chandler & Cleocatra.

Regina Rioux Gonzalez is an exhibiting artist and fabricator of creatures. She is obsessed with fairy tales, felt, and guerrilla vegetables. Regina received her Bachelor's Degree in art from California State University, Northridge, and her Master's Degree in fine art from Claremont Graduate University. After finishing her education, she taught art to children and adults. Currently she spends her days generating income, and her nights enmeshed in a world populated by crocheted churros sporting sombreros; vegetables wielding weapons; bins filled with yarn; felt and sordid errata: making art; assembling creatures; and devising ways to unleash them on an unsuspecting world via her website www.monstercrochet.com and blog http://monstercrochet.blogspot.com.

Deborah Grossman would like to teach the world to crochet. As a start, she teaches at one of her local yarn stores in Santa Fe, New Mexico. In addition, she recently taught her son's elementary school class to crochet. Deborah's first published designs appear in *Cool Crocheted Hats* (Lark, 2006). You can see her other work at www.dulcineadesign.com. Deborah would like to thank her mother, a compulsive knitter, for passing along the needlecraft bug.

Jennifer Hansen lives in Fremont, California, where she is a full-time designer, teacher, and writer. Her innovative work has been featured in various books and magazines including *Vogue Knitting*, *Interweave Crochet*, and *The Happy Hooker*. She also publishes designs through her company, Stitch Diva Studios. Stitch Diva Studios patterns are available for download, and may also be purchased at yarn stores nationwide. You can visit Stitch Diva Studios online at www.stitchdiva.com to view more of Jennifer's designs.

Tammy Hildebrand shares her home in North Carolina with her husband and best friend, George, along with their two daughters, Chelsea, and Shelby. She was taught how to crochet by her second grade teacher, Gail Crooks. Tammy designs full-time, with many of her creations appearing in various books and magazines. As the only crocheter in her family, she hopes to one day get a hook in everyone's hand (this means you, Mom). She is currently the mentor coordinator for the Crochet Guild of America and also serves on the professional development board.

Kalpna Kapoor lives with her husband and three kids in Santa Clarita, California. Her mother taught her to knit and crochet at a very young age. Her designs have been published in several books including *The New Crochet: 40 Wonderful Wearables* (Lark, 2005), and *Fabulous Crocheted Ponchos: New Styles, New Looks, New Yarns* (Lark, 2005). Kalpna owns Craft-Creations Knitting Studios in Santa Clarita, and teaches both knitting and crochet workshops. You can visit her website at www.knittingandcrochet.com to view more of her designs as well as a wide selection of fine yarns from around the world.

Gwen Blakley Kinsler, founder and past President of the Crochet Guild of America, is a designer and teacher who is committed to sharing her passion for crochet with anyone, especially children. Co-author of *Kids Can Do It Crocheting* (Kids Can Press, 2003), Gwen is currently busy covering her world in crochet one stitch at a time! Visit her website at www.crochetqueen.com.

Kim Lewis is a relative newcomer to knitting and crochet, having learned from her Aunt Jean and her friend Debbie, about four years ago. She is now the proud owner of an embarrassingly large yarn stash, some of which overflows from her bathtub. She and her yarn stash live in Keller, Texas, with cats Mia, Pippa, and Jasper, dog Rusty, and her very understanding and tolerant husband, Rodney.

Sharon Mann's passion is to design with needle, thread, and yarn. She infuses her love of traditional needlecraft with other craft techniques to produce dimensional and novel projects. Currently, her artistic endeavors include crochet, knitting, fiber, and embellishment beading. Sharon lives knee deep in threads and yarn in Las Vegas, Nevada, with her husband Gary. See more of her work at www.sharonmanndesigns.com.

Donna May created crochet designs for over 40 years before submitting her first design for publication. The design was accepted; and since then, she has provided designs for Lark Books, DRG, ASN, yarn companies, and various magazines. She loves crochet because it's a malleable art that fits fluctuating moods, tastes, and needs. Inspired by her grandchildren, she is currently designing a line for babies and children.

Ever since her grandmother taught her to crochet when she was a young girl, **Marty Miller** has been designing patterns for herself and others. Her comfortable, unique garments and accessories have been widely published in magazines and books, including *The New Crochet* (Lark, 2005), *Fabulous Crocheted Ponchos* (Lark, 2005), *The Michaels Book of Needlecrafts* (Lark, 2005) and *Cool Crocheted Hats* (Lark, 2006). In addition to teaching crochet classes both locally and nationally, Marty is now the Professional Development Chairperson for the Crochet Guild of America. Her grandmother would be so proud!

Sharleen Morco lives in California and is majoring in photography at Sacramento State. When she's not clicking away with her camera, she can often be found with a crochet hook and a ball of yarn. Sharleen is a self-taught crocheter who finds inspiration from food and everyday things. You can see more of her work at www.mmm-fruit.com.

Jen Neitzel, a self-taught crocheter, began crocheting as a child. Currently, Jen lives in Portland Oregon, with her husband and son. She owns two small businesses, DIY Lounge, offering creative classes taught by artists and designers (www.diylounge.com), and Knot Ugly Designs, a crochet and knit business (www. knotugly.com). Jen works with crochet designer Kim State. Their shrug pattern was published in *Stitch and Bitch: The Happy Hooker*. Both women are moms and yarn renegades!

Catherine Peterson currently resides in Spokane, Washington, with too much yarn, too many cats, and two Volkswagens. Her mother taught her to crochet several years ago, and now Catherine's designs can be found locally, on the web at www.peachick.com, and in publications such as Vickie Howell's upcoming crochet book, *Catwalk Crochet*.

Joy Prescott has been crocheting since she was 16, when she made her first pink and purple granny square, which grew and grew until it became an afghan. She began designing her own patterns a few years later and has been published in books and magazines so many times that she's lost count. For the last several years, Joy has primarily been designing fashion and fashion accessories for DMC, and playing with freeform crochet. She is a member of CGOA, the Puget Sound Crochet Guild, and various Yahoo groups. When she's not working as a technical writer, Joy practices living a sustainable lifestyle in the suburbs of Bellevue, Washington, with her husband and her mostly secondhand yarn collection. Joy also self-publishes crochet patterns, which are available through her website, www.CrochetWithAttitude.com.

Phyllis Sandford is a freelance designer. Her love of fibers has drawn her to crocheting, knitting, felting, needlefelting, and the needle arts. She has had numerous articles published in magazines, books, and project sheets. Phyllis is a member of TKGA and CGOA. A grandmother of 10, she has been busy teaching the older ones to crochet and knit.

Nanette Seale lives in central Arizona, where she enjoys life surrounded by yarn, pets, and kids (not necessarily in that order), and spends as much time as possible creating crochet designs. She learned to crochet at age 11, but for the most part is self-taught. Nanette is a professional member of CGOA, and has been designing for almost 20 years. Her grandbabies are the current source of inspiration for her designs; especially four-year-old Emily, who crochets with her Grandma Nan every chance she gets.

Pam Shore learned to crochet at age 12. Inspired by the resurgence of crochet in the 1970s, her addiction to crochet grew rapidly, as did her collection of hooks and books. Since 1995, the Crochet Guild of America and its annual conferences have fueled her creativity by exposing her to many other passionate crocheters and fiber artists. She will be eternally grateful to CGOA.

Myra Wood has over 25 years of professional art experience as a graphic designer and illustrator for the commercial and entertainment industries in Los Angeles, New York, and Philadelphia. Returning to her childhood love of crochet and crafts over 10 years ago, she now designs and teaches for craft and fiber-arts books and magazines. Her primary focus is her love of all things freeform, especially freeform crochet and beading. She has appeared as a guest on several episodes of DIY's Knitty Gritty and Uncommon Threads. Myra is also the moderator and coordinator for annual shows and an online list for the International Freeform Fiberart Guild with over 1000 members. She is also a member of the Crochet Guild of America and volunteers for their web design committee. Visit: www.myrawood.com and www.woodworksart.com to see her full range of work and www.60-odd.com to learn more about freeform crochet.

Stitches & Techniques

Hook in one hand, yarn in the other, and ready to stitch? This section is your guide to crochet stitches and techniques used in the projects. Included are many of the basics that you're probably already familiar with, but there are a few more exotic stitches and techniques that you might want to take a peek at. So whether for a quick refresher, or to learn a new stitch or method, refer to this section as needed. The stitches are in alpha order, and the name of a stitch is followed by its abbreviation.

BASIC CROCHET STITCHES

The stitches below are some of the more basic stitches that you'll find in many of the project patterns.

Chain (ch)

1. Make a slipknot.

2. Slide the slipknot onto your hook.

3. Holding your hook, bring the yarn over the hook from back to front. Bring the yarn through the loop (lp) on your hook.

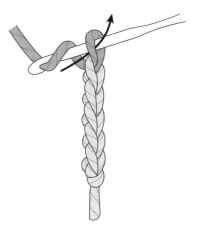

4. Repeat that series of steps over and over again to make a chain.

Double Crochet Stitch (dc)

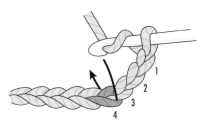

1. Make a foundation chain of any number of stitches. Bring the yarn over the hook and insert the hook into the fourth chain from the hook.

2. Bring the yarn over the hook and pull the yarn through the chain stitch. You'll have three loops on your hook.

3. Bring the yarn over the hook and draw the yarn through the first two loops on the hook. You'll have two loops on your hook.

4. Bring the yarn over the hook once more, then pull the yarn through the last two loops on your hook. You've completed one double crochet stitch. You'll have one loop left on your hook to start your next double crochet.

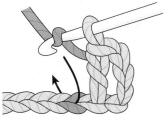

5. Bring the yarn over your hook, insert your hook in the next stitch, and continue across the row. At the end of the row, turn your work and chain three to make your turning chain.

Half Double Crochet (hdc)

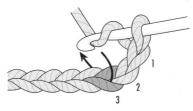

1. Make a foundation chain of any number of stitches. Bring the yarn over the hook, locate the third chain stitch from the hook, and insert the hook in the chain.

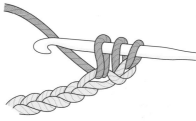

2. Bring the yarn over the hook and catch it with the hook. Pull the hook through the chain. You should have three loops on the hook.

3. Bring the yarn over the hook, catch the yarn with the hook, and pull it through the three loops on the hook.

4. You will have one loop left on the hook. You've created one half double crochet stitch. Yarn over and insert the hook in the next chain, and repeat the sequence across the row.

Single Crochet (sc)

1. Begin with a foundation chain of any number of stitches. Find the second chain stitch from the crochet hook. Insert the point of the hook under the two top loops of the chain stitch.

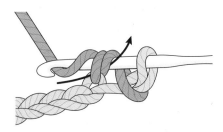

2. Bring the yarn over (yo) the crochet hook, catch the yarn, and pull it through the loop on the hook. You will now have two loops on your hook.

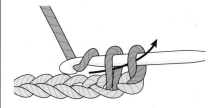

3. Bring the yarn over the hook again, grab the yarn with the hook, and pull the yarn through both loops. You've completed your first single crochet stitch.

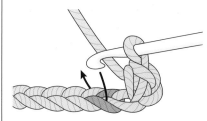

4. Insert your hook in the next chain stitch and repeat the steps to create another single crochet.

Slip Stitch (sl st)

Insert the hook into any stitch. Bring the yarn over, catch the yarn, and pull the hook through the stitch and the loop on your hook. This completes one slip stitch. You'll have one loop remaining on the hook.

Treble Crochet (tr)

Start with a foundation chain of any number of stitches.

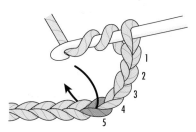

1. Identify the fifth chain stitch from the hook. Bring the yarn over the hook twice.

2. Insert the hook into the fifth chain. Bring the yarn over the hook, catch the yarn, and pull the hook through the chain. You'll have four loops on the hook.

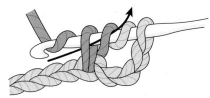

3. Bring the yarn over the hook, catch the yarn, and slide the hook through the first two loops).

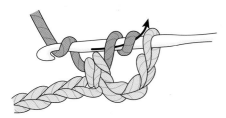

4. Yarn over the hook and draw your yarn through the next two loops on the hook.

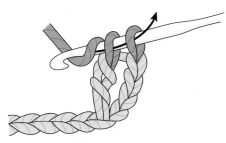

5. Yarn over the hook and draw the yarn through the last two loops on your hook.

6. You will end up with only one loop on your hook. You've completed one treble crochet stitch. Yarn over twice and repeat the steps in the next chain stitch.

SPECIAL STITCHES

The following stitches are not used in every project but are useful to know and fun to experiment with. Refer to this section if the pattern you're working calls for any of these special stitches.

Back-Post Double Crochet (BPdc)

Yarn over, insert hook from back to front then to back, going around the double crochet post, draw up a loop, (yarn over and draw through 2 loops on hook) twice. Skip stitch behind the BPdc.

Cluster (CL)

Yarn over, insert hook in next stitch and draw up a loop about 3/4"/2cm long, yarn over and draw through 2 loops, (yarn over, insert hook in same stitch and draw up a loop about 3/4"/2cm long, yarn over and draw through 2 loops) 3 times, yarn over, draw through all loops on hook.

Double Crochet Decrease (dc2tog)

(Yarn over, insert hook in next stitch and draw up a loop, yarn over and draw through 2 loops on hook) twice, yarn over and draw through all loops on hook.

Double-Faced Single Crochet (dfsc)

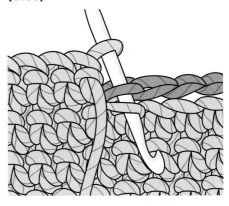

1. Insert hook in back loop of indicated stitch and free loop of corresponding stitch one row below.

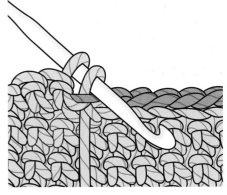

2. Yarn over and draw through both loops.

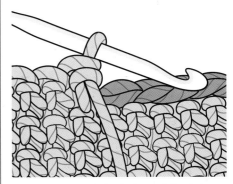

3. Yarn over and draw through both loops on hook.

Extended Single Crochet (esc)

Draw up loop in indicated stitch, yarn over and draw through 1 loop on hook, yarn over and draw through both loops on hook.

Extended Single Crochet Decrease (esc2tog)

Draw up loop in indicated stitch, yarn over and draw through 1 loop on hook, draw up loop in next stitch, yarn over and draw through 1 loop on hook, yarn over and draw through all 3 loops on hook.

Front-Post Double Crochet (FPdc)

Yarn over, insert hook from front to back then to front, going around the double crochet post, draw up a loop, (yarn over and draw through 2 loops on hook) twice. Skip stitch behind the FPdc.

Granule Stitch (no abbreviation)

sc in indicated stitch, draw up loop in the next stitch, ch 3, yarn over and draw through both loops on hook, sc in next stitch.

Half Double Crochet Decrease (hdc2tog)

(Yarn over, insert hook in next stitch and draw up a loop) twice, yarn over and draw through all 5 loops on hook.

Loop Stitch (lpst)

Worked with wrong side of project facing; loops form on right side.

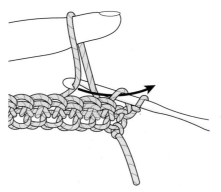

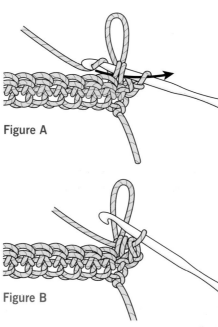

Figure A

Figure B

1. Use the left-hand finger to control the size of the loop. Insert the hook, pick up both threads of the loop, and draw them through.

2. Wrap the yarn over the hook (figure A) and draw through all of the loops on the hook to complete the stitch (figure B).

Petal Stitch (no abbreviation)

(sc, hdc, 3 dc, hdc, sc) in indicated stitch.

Popcorn Stitch (no abbreviation)

5 dc in indicated stitch, drop loop from hook and insert hook in first dc worked and back through dropped loop, yarn over and pull through both stitches, ch 1 to close popcorn.

Shell Stitch (no abbreviation)

(3 dc, ch 3, 3 dc) in indicated stitch.

Single Crochet Decrease (sc2tog)

Insert hook into stitch and draw up a loop, insert hook in next stitch and draw up a loop, yarn over, draw through all loops on hook.

Single Crochet Double Decrease (sc3tog)

Insert hook into stitch and draw up a loop, (insert hook in next stitch and draw up a loop) twice, yarn over, draw through all loops on hook.

Shallow Single Crochet (ssc)

Work as for single crochet except insert hook low into body of each stitch, below all 3 horizontal loops and between both vertical threads.

Shallow Single Crochet Decrease (ssc2tog)

Work as for sc2tog, except insert hook low into body of each stitch, below all 3 horizontal loops and between both vertical threads.

Shallow Single Crochet Double Decrease (ssc3tog)

Work as for sc3tog, except insert hook low into body of each stitch, below all 3 horizontal loops and between both vertical threads.

Wave Pattern

Wave pattern (no abbreviation) – sc in next stitch, hdc in next stitch, dc in next stitch, hdc in next stitch, sc in next stitch.

SPECIAL TECHNIQUES

Refer to the section below if you run across a technique that you're not familiar with.

Changing Color

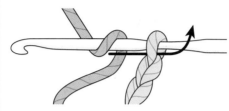

Yarn over with new color, and draw through last loop on hook.

Double Ring Method

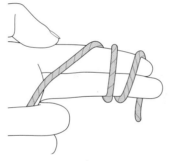

1. Hold yarn a few inches from the end, and wrap it twice around your fingers.

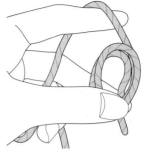

2. Remove the loops from your fingers, holding them and the tail firmly between your middle finger and thumb.

3. Insert hook through center of ring and draw up a loop. Chain 1.

4. Work stitches of first round in the rings.

5. Grip the stitches tightly and pull gently but firmly on tail to tighten one of the loops. Continue pulling to close the second loop.

French Knot

Thread needle and bring from back to front through piece. Wrap yarn around needle 3 times, insert needle back into piece close to where it emerged. Tighten knot.

Invisible Join

Work last single crochet of round. Remove hook from loop. Insert hook under top two loops of first single crochet of round from back to front, and back into dropped loop. Pull loop through single crochet. Chain 1 to begin next round.

Single Crochet Around a Ring (sc around ring)

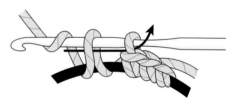

Join with sl st around ring, ch 1, sc in ring.

Acknowledgments

A big thank you to Rags Reborn Eco Chic Boutique (www.ragsreborn.com) and to Dema, proprietress of downtown Asheville's sophisticated Zakya Boutique, for the loan of many of the stylish clothes featured in the photos.

Also, a big standing ovation for hair and makeup artist extraordinaire, E. Scott Thompson, who not only brought to the shoot his usual enthusiasm and myriad of talents, but his own personal collection of outrageous wigs and eyewear. What a treasure you are, Scott!

And to KJ, thanks for responding to my many queries with the patience of a saint and some much appreciated humor.

And lastly, to my lifelong buddy Kim Lewis, thank you for your witty words, constant enthusiasm, and unflagging moral support. You rock!

Index

A

Accessory projects, 76–105
Acknowledgements, 124
Amigurumi, 7, 22, 38
Animals, 7, 22, 25, 38, 58, 106, 110
Appliqués, 96

B

Back-post double crochet stitch, 119
Bags, 6, 78, 86, 88, 92, 100, 103
Balls, 7, 20, 28
Basic stitches, 116
Belts, 73
Bumper sweater, 111

C

Chain stitch, 116
Changing color, 121
Cluster stitch, 119
Coasters, 41
Coffee sleeve, 82

D

Dentures, 109
Designer biographies, 112–115
Double crochet stitch, 116–117
Double ring method, 23, 37, 93, 121
Double crochet decrease stitch, 119
Double-faced single crochet stitch, 119
Double ring method, 121

E

Extended single crochet decrease, 120
Extended single crochet stitch, 120

F

Felting, 40, 41, 43, 64, 80
Flip-flops, 62
Food, crocheted, 10, 13, 30, 33, 107
French knot, 10, 122
Front-post double crochet stitch, 120

G

Gallery, 106–111
Gloves, 70, 107
Gnome, 109
Granule stitch, 120

H

Half double crochet decrease, 120
Half double crochet stitch, 117
Hats, 6, 58, 100, 103

I

Invisible join, 39, 122

K

Kitsch projects, 8–51

L

Leg warmers, 70
Loop stitch, 120

O

Objets d'art, 7
Oven Mitts, 6, 25

P

Petal stitch, 120
Pet toys, 28
Pillows, 7, 36
Place mats, 13
Plastic bags, crocheting with, 100
Polypropylene duct support strap
    or webbing, 87
Popcorn stitch, 120
Potholders, 6, 25, 30
Puffs, 7, 29
Puppets, 44

R

Rock garden, 48

S

Shallow single crochet, 120
Shallow single crochet decrease, 121
Shallow single crochet double
    decrease, 121
Shell stitch, 120
Single crochet around a ring, 122
Single crochet decrease, 120
Single crochet double decrease, 120
Single crochet stitch, 118
Ski Mask, 54
Slip stitch, 118
Special stitches, 119
Stitches, all, 116–122

T

Tea cosy, 108
Techniques, 116–122
Tops, 66
Treble crochet stitch, 118

V

Vinyl yarn, 73

W

Washers, 70
Wave Pattern, 121
Wearable projects, 52–75